THE CHURCH OF THE CATACOMBS

The Introduction to the Surging Life of the Early Church from the Apostles to A. D. 250, Based on Firsthand Accounts

BY WALTER W. OETTING

D1484577

CONCORDIA PUBLISHING HOUSE · SAINT LOUIS, MISSOURI

Acknowledgments

To Cambridge University Press, New York, for quotations from *The Apostolic Tradition of Hippolytus*, edited by Burton Scott Easton; to the Newman Press, Westminster, Maryland, for quotations from *Ancient Christian Writers, Vol. 28, Tertullian: On Penance and on Purity*, translated by William P. Le Saint; to The Westminster Press, Philadelphia, for quotations from *Early Christian Fathers, Vol. I, LCC*, edited by Cyril Richardson, 1953; to Wm. B. Eerdmans Publishing Company for quotations from *Irenaeus, Against Heresies, Vol. I, The Ante-Nicene Fathers*, edited by Alexander Roberts and James Donaldson, 1950; to S. P. C. K., London, for quotations from *Some Authentic Acts of the Early Martyrs*, by E. C. E. Owen; to Oxford University Press, New York, for quotations from *Documents of the Christian Church*, edited by Henry Bettenson, 1947.

Second Printing 1970, Slightly Revised

Concordia Publishing House, St. Louis, Missouri

Library of Congress Catalog Card No. 64-24277

MANUFACTURED IN THE UNITED STATES OF AMERICA

Dedicated to
Rose Marie
and
Our Three Sons

Foreword

In this volume, modest in length but important in content, Walter W. Oetting takes the reader right into the early church. He exposes us to a new world. The ancient community suddenly comes alive through authentic voices of the period. He opens up to us the excitement of early Christianity and uncovers for us the roots of our church.

He thus restores to us the sense of real continuity with classical Christendom, a continuity which the Reformation stressed and understood.

The author delivered the manuscript of this "inside early church" report for publication four days before his sudden death on February 25, 1964. This final literary contribution of a youthful historian and promising teacher of theology will enrich the lives of a new generation as they discover their ancient heritage.

Gilbert A. Thiele
Concordia Seminary
St. Louis, Missouri

June 29, 1964
Feast of Saints Peter and Paul, Apostles

Contents

THE CHURCH OF THE CATACOMBS

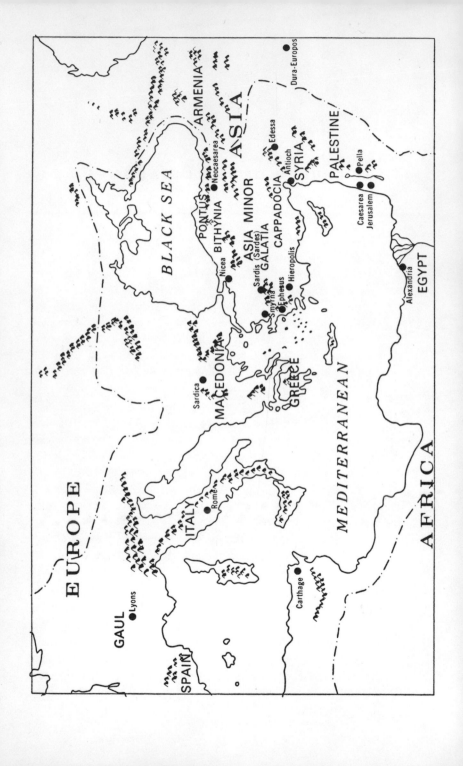

Introduction

This book is an attempt to describe what took place in the Christian communities after the period that is described by the literature of the New Testament. Basically it analyzes the last decades of the first through the first decades of the third century. The last specifically historical material included in the New Testament is the Acts of the Apostles, which reaches the first years of the sixties; however, the composition of the Gospels and some of the letters falls into the period after 60. We have attempted to pick up the story where these materials leave off.

We have treated early Christianity topically rather than either purely chronologically or geographically. The themes discussed take up issues that still confront the church in our own generation, questions concerning mission work, modes of worship, polity of congregations and synods, the church's effort to speak the Gospel in terms relevant and meaningful, the orientation of the church toward society, and the relationship of Christianity to the state. We have limited value judgments and applications to the minimum. This is something the reader must do for himself either alone or in discussion with others.

We ought to say something about the quotations from early Christian documents. If the reader checks with the original he will find that the translations are often not literal. We have tried to reproduce the meaning of the author accurately without being bound to his sentence structure. We hope that this will make the meaning of the quotation clearer. We certainly owe very much to translations of the church fathers available in English, especially those in *The Library of Christian Classics* and in the *Ante-Nicene Fathers.*

There are so many people who helped in the production of this work, in many cases unknowingly, that it would be impossible to mention them. We had thought of dedicating the book to the many students whose "depth studies" and class discussion have been a great stimulation. Certainly we want to recognize them here. Special thanks are due to my colleague Philip Schroeder, who was kind enough to apply his splendid knowledge of language to the revisions of this work, and also to my beloved wife for her patience.

I. MISSION

BEGINNINGS

Christianity is a faith — a faith that is based on the activity of God in history. The writer to the Hebrews began his letter, "In many and various ways God spoke of old to our fathers by the prophets; but in these last days He has spoken to us by a Son. . . ." This was God's unique intervention into history for the salvation of man. Jesus was born at Bethlehem in Judea in the reign of Caesar Augustus. He was executed during the reign of Tiberius some 30 years later. His crime in the eyes of the Romans was apparently that He called Himself "a king." The grave did not hold Jesus. He arose "on the third day" and appeared to His followers. This was the beginning of the Christian religion.

Jesus spent His life working in one province of the Roman Empire, a "worldwide" state covering the area surrounding the Mediterranean Sea. Jesus lived during a crucial period of this empire's history. Caesar Augustus' reign was the beginning of the imperial period. As Rome slowly encompassed the Mediterranean, the old city-state governmental and social structures broke down, and Italy was plunged into a century of civil and social war. It was Augustus who brought peace and justice out of this chaos. And it was precisely at this time — a long-sought-after period of peace — that Jesus taught. Peter characterized Jesus' activities in the short phrase, "He went about doing good." If He went about visiting the socially disinherited as well as people of influence, He also taught whoever was willing to listen. His language was not learned but rather evidenced the quality of abandon. He did not generally quote other sources as authority, and when He did He had no scruples about suggesting that Moses said certain things only because the people would not have accepted the whole counsel of God. One poet has characterized his language as "gigantesque." Jesus could call His followers "the salt of the earth," and refer to Himself as "the door." He told the man whose eye caused him to sin to "pluck it out." He reproved people who were so concerned with the speck in their neighbor's eye that they didn't see the log protruding out of their own; He rebuked teachers whose lives seemed as pure as the whitewash on a tomb but whose true, inner qualities could better be likened to "dead men's bones."

It wasn't merely the way Jesus said things that struck people but also what He said. Mark summarized His preaching as, "The time is fulfilled, and the kingdom of God is at hand; repent, and believe in the Gospel" (Mark 1:14 RSV). "Repent!" Jesus insisted that the people to whom He was speaking were hiding from God's presence. Instead of listening to what God had really said — "Love the Lord your God with all your heart, soul, and mind; and your neighbor as yourself" — they were following the rules by which they interpreted this Law of God to suit their own convenience, He claimed. They defined the meaning of "love" and of "neighbor" to the point where they could claim to be doing the Law. Jesus distinguished between what the people had been taught and what God had actually commanded. He called them from hiding behind their own systems of morality into the living presence of God with the word "Repent." But at the same time He announced that the kingdom of God was present in His person. The prophets had said that in His own time God would descend and reign among men. This reign, Jesus claimed, was being inaugurated in Himself. This is the Gospel, the good news, to which Mark referred.

His disciples spread this message of "Repent, and believe in the Gospel" wherever they went in the Roman Empire and beyond, always insisting that they "behold His glory, the glory as of the Only-begotten of the Father, full of grace and truth" (John 1:14). The letters of Paul, Peter, John, and James breathed this message. They confidently preached that "there is forgiveness with God" since Jesus Christ fought the forces of darkness and won! "God was in Christ reconciling the world to Himself, not counting their trespasses against them" (2 Cor. 5:19 RSV). It was the message of victory over death through the resurrection of Jesus Christ from the dead that summarized their mission to men. Easter was *the* great feast day of the early Christians because it was on this day that they celebrated their victory over death.

JEWS AND GENTILES

Christianity spread over the Roman Empire from the cities of Jerusalem and Antioch.

To one who looked at it from the outside the church in Jerusalem appeared like merely another sect within Judaism. Yet the Christians differed fundamentally from their Jewish brethren, even though they were themselves Jews, when they accepted Jesus as the Messiah (the Christ) and taught that salvation would not come through doing the Law but had already come in Jesus, the Christ, as the fulfillment of God's gracious promise.

Believing that they represented authentic Judaism, the earliest Christians closely related their lives to the religious life of their neighbors. The Christians were under the jurisdiction of the Jewish Sanhedrin. When Peter and John preached in Jerusalem, they were forced to defend themselves before the religious and civil courts of the Jews. Many of the early Christians continued to worship in the synagog and were faithful to some of the ceremonial laws of Judaism; they fasted twice a week, attended temple and synagog, observed dietetic regulations, practiced circumcision, and in many cases probably continued to observe the Sabbath.

The gap between Christian and non-Christian Jew was widened with the persecution of the Christians in Jerusalem by the anti-Christian Jews. It was in this persecution, probably in the year 32, that we hear of the first Christian martyr, Stephen. As a result of this persecution it seems that a number of Christians fled from Jerusalem and settled in the Greek city of Antioch, where Christianity was preached to the uncircumcised.

The city of Antioch was very important for the spread of the Christian Gospel. Its population was made up of people from many lands. Since Jews had been settled there by the successors of Alexander the Great when they refused to comply with pagan religious regulations, there was a large Jewish settlement in Antioch by the time of our Lord. There were also many proselytes in this city, Greeks who had been fully converted to Judaism, as well as to the so-called "God-fearers," or "devout men" (Acts 10:2), Greeks who accepted the God of the Jews but not the ceremonial of Judaism. The Greek-speaking Jews, or "Hellenists" (Acts 6:1), and the Gentiles who worshiped with them in the synagogs in Antioch provided the fertile ground for the Christian appeal outside the confines of strict Judaism. As a result, both circumcised and uncircumcised Christians worshiped and ate together for the first time.

Since this type of integrated church represented a new turn for Christianity, the church in Jerusalem sent Barnabas to check on these activities. Barnabas was a Christian Jew from Cyprus and so fit well into the environment of Antioch. He also encouraged Paul, a Jewish convert to Christianity from Greek Tarsus, to help in the work at Antioch. (Acts 11:19-26)

Preaching the Gospel to the Gentiles was continued especially through the work of the apostle Paul. Commissioned by the congregation in Antioch, Paul and Barnabas carried the Christian Gospel through Asia Minor. Dividing into two teams, Barnabas took John Mark with him to his home in Cyprus, where they contined their efforts; Paul, accompanied by Silas, covered the same territory again in Asia Minor but then went on into Greece. Paul was ultimately able to reach Rome. Because he did not require his converts to become Jews before they became Christians, Paul aroused the displeasure of some Jewish Christians in the church at Jerusalem. (Acts 15:1-5)

To settle this question a number of the early Christian leaders met in Jerusalem. They agreed that Christianity was more than a sect in Judaism but assumed that the followers of Jesus would remain loyal to the revealed Word of God — the Torah (Acts 15:6 ff.). Observing the Sabbath, circumcision, and the food laws was not demanded of all followers of Jesus Christ. Gentile Christians were merely required to refrain from strangled meat, food offered to idols (cf. 1 Cor. 10:25 ff.), blood, and unchastity (Acts 15:28, 29). But it was not decided at Jerusalem how a Christian who had come out of the Jewish tradition should act in a congregation that was predominantly Greek. Would it be possible for a Jewish Christian to forsake Jewish regulations if he lived among Greeks who did not know this heritage? This continued to cause discussion in the early church. It seems that Peter and Paul, for example, had difficulty with this issue (Gal. 2:11-16). It was Paul's position that Christians must forbear one another. (Rom. 14:1—15:6; 1 Cor. 8:1—9:27)

The leader of the church in Jerusalem was James the brother of our Lord. Attempting to mediate between Paul, the missionary among the Gentiles, and those zealots in the church at Jerusalem who insisted that all the Gentiles converted to Christianity be circumcised, James did not insist on the full acceptance of all the traditions of Judaism but at the same time advocated that the church avert any break between herself and the ancient people of God (Acts 21: 18 ff.). James was a blend of Jewish piety and of the belief that Jesus is the Messiah.

These were the years in which the Jewish rebellion against the Romans which culminated in the destruction of Jerusalem in the year 70 [1] was gaining momentum. Since the day when the Jews were able to win back their freedom from the Seleucids under the leadership of the Maccabees in the middle of the second century B. C., only to lose it again to the Roman Pompey in the middle of the sixties B. C., especially the Zealots continued to propagandize and to terrorize

[1] See the description in Flavius Josephus, *Wars of the Jews,* V, 9— VI, 9.

in the hope of freedom from foreign domination. When the Roman governor died (62) and the new governor had not yet arrived, the Sanhedrin in Jerusalem took power. Venting their zeal on the small Christian group, they accused James of blasphemy and demanded that he go before the people and tell them that Jesus was not the Messiah. Instead of disclaiming his belief he confessed that Jesus was indeed the Anointed of God. As a result of this "blasphemy" James was thrown from a cliff and stoned to death.[2] Because the Christians in Jerusalem sensed the fearful events about to take place and because the Jewish authorities were less and less tolerant of their activities, the Christians fled from Jerusalem to the Gentile city of Pella in the years 62—70. Eusebius tells us, "The people of the church in Jerusalem, as a result of a revelation given to worthy men there, departed from the city before the war to dwell in a city of Perea called Pella." [3]

When these Christians fled to the east of the Jordan they established communities of faith that did not remain in contact with the congregations established by Paul and other missionaries. These communities existed in isolated areas into the fifth century.

Since most of them were Jewish Christians, they developed a form of Christianity that attempted to preserve much of the ritual of Judaism as part of their faith. Accepting the "Judaizing" position as more or less the correct one in opposition to Paul, they continued to follow certain Jewish practices such as circumcision and the Sabbath observance. They did, however, celebrate the Eucharist on Sunday and accepted Jesus as the promised Messiah; but they claimed that He was born in a natural way, receiving divine power in His baptism. Our Lord's baptism and His resurrection played most important roles in their theology. One of these communities took the name "Nazarenes" (Matt. 2:23; Acts 24:5). This was a name given early to the followers of

---

[2] Josephus, *Antiquities of the Jews,* XX, ix, 1.

[3] Eusebius, *Ecclesiastical History,* III, v, 3.

Jesus. Another group called themselves "Ebionites," a word meaning "Poor," which they presumably applied to themselves after the words of Jesus in the Sermon on the Mount, "Blessed are the poor in spirit."

INTO ALL THE WORLD

It isn't known who established the churches in Rome, Alexandria, Carthage, or Lyons, but there were many traditions about the origin of these congregations among the early Christians.

The early church credited Peter and Paul with the founding of the church in Rome. Irenaeus, bishop in Lyons at the end of the second century, wrote about "the tradition of that very great, oldest, and well-known church, founded and established [at Rome] by those two most glorious apostles, Peter and Paul . . ." and used the expression, "When the blessed apostles had founded and established the church [in Rome] . . ."[4] This is one of those traditions that doesn't square with the fact that St. Paul wrote to the Roman Christians before he was in Rome himself and that when he came to Rome for the first time he was met by the "brethren" (Rom. 1:10; Acts 28:15-28). The best explanation of the origin of the Christian community in Rome is that Jewish Christians traveling in the area and settling there founded it.

This congregation became the uniquely honored church in Christendom by the beginning of the second century. A number of reasons are given to explain this. It was the first church to suffer persecution by the Roman government. Nero (64) and probably Domitian (95) persecuted Christians there. It was generally assumed in the early church that both Peter and Paul were martyred there during these persecutions. Clement, a presbyter-bishop in Rome c. 95, wrote:

> "Let us set before our eyes the noble apostles: Peter, who by reason of wicked jealousy not only once or twice but frequently endured suffering and thus, bearing his witness,

---

[4] *Against Heresies,* III, iii, 1, 2. Adapted from C. Richardson, *Early Christian Fathers* (Philadelphia: Westminster Press, 1953), p. 372.

went to the glorious place which he merited. By reason of
rivalry and contention Paul showed how to win the prize
for patient endurance. Seven times he was in chains; he was
exiled and stoned, became a herald [of the Gospel] in East
and West, and won the noble renown which his faith merited." [5]

These two facts, coupled with the imperial position of Rome
and the reputation for charity and hospitality that the congregation possessed, help to explain why it was revered as
preeminent very early in the church.

There was a saying that "all roads lead to Rome." When
trouble arose in Corinth, one of the presbyter-bishops in
Rome, probably Clement (c. 95), wrote to that church, as
Paul had previously, suggesting that they return to the Rule
of Obedience. Ignatius, bishop of Antioch c. 110, was taken
to Rome to be martyred. Many Christian intellectuals from
various parts of the world, men like Justin Martyr, Marcion,
and Valentine, spent some time in Rome as teachers. All
of the evidence that we have points to the conclusion that this
church was a "vast multitude" already at the beginning of
the second century.[6] By the middle of the third century the
Roman church had 1 bishop, 46 elders, 7 deacons, as many
subdeacons, 42 acolytes, 52 readers, exorcists, and doorkeepers, and over 1,500 widows and poor persons under its
care.[7]

The beginnings of the church in Egypt are lost in the mist
of time. Early Christians believed that Mark or Barnabas
founded the church in Alexandria.[8] The limited evidence that
we have concerning Christianity there in the second century
indicates that it was in part an attempt to find a philosophical
basis for combining various religious traditions. A letter
supposedly from the hand of the Emperor Hadrian (c. 125)
tells about the religious life that he experienced in Alexandria:

---

[5] *1 Clement,* 5. Adapted from Richardson, p. 46.
[6] Cornelius Tacitus, *Annals,* XV, 44; *1 Clement,* 6.
[7] Eusebius, *Ecclesiastical History,* VI, xliii, 11.
[8] See Acts 15:39 and Eusebius, *Eccl. Hist.,* II, xvi, 1.

"Egypt, which you praised to me so warmly, my dear
Servianus, I found altogether frivolous, unstable, and shift-
ing with every breath of rumor. There those who worshiped
Serapis are Christians, and those who called themselves
bishops of Christ are devoted to Serapis. There is in that
country no ruler of the synagog of the Jews, no Samaritan,
no Christian priest who is not astrologer, soothsayer, or
apothecary. Even the renowned Patriarch when he comes to
Egypt is compelled by some to worship Serapis, by others
to worship Christ." [9]

This type of religious thought was common in Egypt among
the Jews. According to tradition, Ptolemy, the ruler of
Egypt 285—247 B. C., had the Hebrew Scriptures translated
into Greek in order that they might become part of the over-
all religious life of the Egyptians. This version is called the
Septuagint. The Alexandrian Jew Philo felt he could bring
the Hebrew prophets and the Greek philosophers into conformity by finding the supposed "hidden" meaning in the
Old Testament. This type of interpretation is called "alle-
gory."

Among the Christians Valentine (c. 135) tried to get behind the words of Scripture to this "spiritual" meaning. What
the Scriptures really taught, he claimed, was a form of religion that was quite compatible with the other religions of
Egypt. He suggested, for example, that there is only one
God, but this one God has no name. Ultimately then, the
many names applied to divine beings do not refer to many
gods but are simply names by which the one God is worshiped. They portrayed Christ as a Savior sent from the
hitherto unknown God to bring saving knowledge to men
about God. Since the word for knowledge in Greek is *gnosis,*
this type of Christianity is called Gnosticism. (See pages 54
to 56)

About 180 a teacher by the name of Pantaenus came to
Alexandria. He had been a Stoic philosopher before he was
converted to Christianity. The school that flourished under
Pantaenus in Egypt, one of the most famous of Christian
schools in the early church, also illustrates the syncretistic

---

[9] Flavius Vopiscus, *Life of Saturninus,* 7—8.

nature of Christianity in Egypt. It was basically a school to instruct in the Christian Gospel young and old, educated and uneducated. But attached to this school, though not identical with it, was a course of instruction that went all the way from basic grammar to the highest speculations in Christian philosophy. It seems that geography, archaeology, astronomy, and medicine were also studied here.[10] This school was open to any interested pagan even if he or she was not interested in becoming a Christian. Here a long succession of theologians taught that true philosophy would ultimately lead to the Christian faith and that all the arts and sciences were valuable to the believer as tools to elucidate the Christian Gospel. The disciple of Pantaenus was Clement, the successor of Clement was Origen, and Origen was the teacher of many of the bishops from that part of the world who were at the Council of Nicaea in 325. These individuals can be credited with bringing Egyptian Christianity into the mainstream of the Christian tradition.

Of the church's origin in Carthage in Africa and Lyons in southern France we know even less. It is probable that Christians either from Ephesus in Asia Minor or from Rome were the first to bring Christianity to Carthage in North Africa. Tertullian, a presbyter there toward the end of the second century, is the first Christian whom we know by name in that church. But by this time there were so many Christians in North Africa that Tertullian could threaten the local Roman ruler with rebellion if he continued to persecute Christians: "We are a people of yesterday and yet we have filled every place belonging to you — cities, islands, castles, towns, assemblies, your very camp, your tribes, companies, palace, senate, forum. We leave you only your temples. We can count your armies; our numbers in a single province will be greater." [11]

We first hear about the church at Lyons in France about 170 through the writings of Irenaeus, a bishop in that church.

---

[10] Gregory Thaumaturgus, *Panegyric to Origen,* 8.

[11] Tertullian, *Apology,* I.

By this time there were many Christians in this area and more than one congregation. When Emperor Marcus Aurelius persecuted this church c. 170, there were some 50 martyrs.

Toward the end of the second century and in the beginning of the third the church also continued its eastward spread. Around 160 we hear of a teacher by the name of Tatian in Edessa in eastern Syria. Tatian was known for his *Diatessaron,* in which he attempted to combine the Four Gospels into one account. It remained the standard reading in the worship of the church in that part of the world into the fifth century.

The most famous missionary in this early period of the church's history was Gregory Thaumaturgus. Gregory was born around 213 at Neocaesarea in Pontus. He studied under Origen at Caesarea in Palestine, where he was converted to the Christian faith. While bishop of Neocaesarea, he did mission work in Cappadocia, where he converted many pagans to Christianity, among them Macrina, the grandmother of the great fourth-century theologians Gregory of Nyssa and Basil of Caesarea. Many stories were told concerning his ability to work miracles. At daybreak men, women, and children suffering from demon possession and disease would gather at his door. As he healed these people he would talk to them about the Gospel, advise them about their troubles, and discuss various religious problems with the inquirer. Gregory of Nyssa wrote that it was "above all for this that he drew many numbers to hear his preaching. . . . His discourse would astonish their hearing, and the wonders he performed would astonish their sight."

By the year 250 Christianity had spread to the limits of the known world. We hear legends about it in England but know little more. We hear about it in areas to the east of Armenia, even in India and China, but know almost nothing about it. Two facts, however, become clear. First, the church spread rapidly over a wide geographical area increasing phenomenally in numbers at the same time. Second, this work was done by ordinary Christians. We know of no missionary societies; we hear nothing of organized effort. Wherever Christians went doing their regular tasks, the pagan saw a different kind of individual and heard the rumors about "the Savior." The spread of Christianity followed the trade routes. In the Middle Ages we hear of many individuals like St. Patrick in Ireland and St. Ansgar in Scandinavia; outside of Gregory we know few missionaries of the early church by name.

When the early Christians themselves recount how they learned of the Gospel, they usually confess that their faith was the result of casual contact with that "way of life." Gregory the missionary claimed that there were many influences in his conversion, but especially the influence of his teacher Origen. "Everything seemed to push me . . . surface reasons. Less obvious, but more important for my salvation was the fellowship with this man. Where I was blind he guided me. He taught me the truth concerning the Word." And again he wrote, "It was like a spark dropping into my inmost soul and catching fire there. A love toward the Word Himself . . . and love toward this man, His friend and representative. . . . I was induced to give up all my plans for education, my pride in legal study, my family and home . . . I had only one love, to study theology under this god-like man." [12] Gregory came to study in Caesarea and happened to find a Christian teacher. Minucius Felix described how Octavius told Caecilius about his Christianity in casual conversation. Justin Martyr was accosted by an old man along the seashore who explained the Old Testament to him. Justin recalled that he was converted to the faith when he saw people willing to die for it in the arena. The pagan Celsus scoffed at the workers in wool and leather, the rustic and ignorant persons who spread Christianity. The work was not done by people who called themselves missionaries but by rank-and-file members. The least among men, even the unknown, are indeed the greatest in the kingdom of heaven.

---

[12] Gregory Thaumaturgus, *Panegyric to Origen*, 5.

II. WORSHIP

If you had asked, "Where is the church?" in any important city of the ancient world where Christianity had penetrated in the first century, you would have been directed to a group of worshiping people gathered in a house. There was no special building or other tangible wealth with which to associate "church," only people! A pagan critic of Christianity, Celsus (c. 170), reproached the Christians for their lack of "temples" and "images." Origen simply replied that all of this was unnecessary for true religion and that Christians could worship their God anywhere.[1]

When Justin Martyr (c. 150) was executed because of his Christian faith, the Roman official asked him to reveal the homes where the Christians worshiped. Justin answered, "Where each wills and can. Do you really think that we all meet in the same place?" The Prefect became more specific, "Tell me, where do *you* meet, in what place do you gather your disciples?" Justin's final comment is indicative, "I lodge above the house of Martin . . . and during all this time I have known no other place of meeting but this house." [2] In Jerusalem the first Christians worshiped in the house of John Mark (Acts 12:12). Paul often referred to the worship that took place in the homes of various individuals (1 Cor. 16:19; Rom. 16:5; Col. 4:15). These places received no other consecration than the worship and teaching that took place there.

[1] *Against Celsus*, VIII, 17, 18.
[2] *Acts of Justin and His Companions*, 3.

Christians sometimes used synagogs, centers of Jewish communities all over the Roman world. Jesus Himself went to the synagog in Nazareth "as was His custom" (Mark 14: 49). Paul usually began his preaching in these centers (Acts 13:5, 14, 42, 43). Peter and John also attended the temple in Jerusalem for afternoon prayers. (Acts 3:1)

In Rome Christians sometimes worshiped in burial caves under the city called catacombs. These catacombs were natural caves that intersect the area on which Rome is built. It is estimated that there are 550 miles of these caves under Rome today. The Christians found these to be natural places for burial. In the East the tombs were usually cut into rock. These caves were an obvious substitute. The bodies of the dead were placed in cavities along the tunnel walls and especially in shelflike openings in the large chambers. The largest chambers held about 50 people. The tunnels from chamber to chamber were very narrow — perhaps three feet wide. For this reason it is improbable that Christians used these caves for regular worship at any time. It is certain, however, that certain ceremonies, especially celebrations of the Eucharist, were held by small groups in connection with the burial and remembrance of the dead.

The first traces of special places for worship occur in the writings of Clement of Alexandria (c. 200), who pointed out that "church" could refer both to the worshiping group and to a special building (*Stromateis,* VII, 29). Not until the middle of the third century did Christians begin to build special buildings for worship in great numbers. It is probable that this building began under the protection of the Persian empire to encourage the Christians to be loyal to it rather than to Rome. In the third century Persia or Palmyra controlled much of Asia Minor and Syria. The first archaeological evidence of a church building proper dates from about 256 in Dura Europa, a town on the Euphrates River. About the same time a church building was erected in the city of Antioch, which was also under Persian domination. After the year 300 many church buildings, generally in the East, were destroyed in the persecution of Diocletian.

The early Christians were not particularly interested in religious art either. As late as 315 the council meeting at Elvira in Spain legislated against pictures in churches "lest the paintings on the wall be worshiped and adored." Interpreting the First Commandment to mean that any representation of God is idolatry and/or blasphemy, early Christian writers generally condemned any artistic representation of the deity and limited themselves to decorative art such as geometric designs. It is interesting, however, that notwithstanding these many condemnations, the Christians in Rome filled their burial catacombs with extensive religious art, including human figures. Usually of flat lines with no architectural feeling or sense of sensuous beauty, the figures symbolized the faith and hope of Christians as expressed in the words: "By His [God's] great mercy we have been born anew to a living hope . . . and to an inheritance which is imperishable, undefiled, and unfading, kept in heaven for you . . . (1 Peter 1:3, 4 RSV). The paintings of the catacombs depict events from Old and New Testament that testify to the intervention of God in history for the salvation of man. The stories of Jonah, Noah's ark, Daniel in the lions' den, the sacrifice of Isaac, the raising of Lazarus, and the Good Shepherd were among the favorites.

FORMS AND REGULATIONS

There was more than one liturgy or form of worship in the early church. One historian writes, "The history of Catholic Christianity during the first centuries is the history of a progressive standardization of a diversity which had its origin in the Apostolic age." [3] In other words, individual areas had their own liturgies, and the liturgy in any given area changed from one period to the next. There is an obvious accumulation as the liturgy grows in form and depth. To classify these early worship forms as either spontaneous or liturgical is not valid. Both elements were present. When St. Paul wrote

---

[3] Burnett Streeter, *The Primitive Church* (New York: Macmillan, 1929), p. 42.

that each member of the congregation contributed something in the service, "a song of praise, a lesson, a revelation, a tongue, an interpretation" (1 Cor. 14:26), he did not exclude liturgical forms. On the other hand, when standard forms of worship are found developing in some areas, it does not mean the elimination of free expression. The very fact that Christians practiced this spontaneity vitiates any attempt to suggest that one liturgical form was *the* "apostolic liturgy."

More is known about the liturgical life of the church in Rome than elsewhere, especially from the remarks in the *First Apology* of Justin Martyr (150) and from *The Apostolic Tradition* of Hippolytus (c. 200). The work of Justin is the first extended account we have of Christian worship. This account exists only because the pagans accused the Christians of doing all sorts of hideous deeds as part of their worship, including the worship of animals, eating children and drinking their blood, and engaging in various kinds of indecency. In order to show the pagans just how wrong they were and precisely what the Christians did in their assemblies, Justin attached his description of worship to a defense of Christianity which he addressed to the emperor. The information in this *Apology* is augmented by *The Apostolic Tradition* of Hippolytus, a bishop in Rome. He called his book of rules for the worship life of the congregation "apostolic" because he believed that the liturgy with which he was familiar had been used by the apostles. We will divide our description into three sections: Baptism, Teaching and Response, and Eucharist.

BAPTISM

Justin described the baptismal rite: "Those who believe what we teach and are willing to live accordingly are instructed to ask God in prayers and fastings to forgive their past sins. We pray and fast with them. They are brought to a place where there is water and . . . bathed in the name of God the Father and Lord of all, and of our Savior Jesus Christ, and of the Holy Spirit"(*1 Apology,* 61). A manual of instruction and liturgical rules called the *Didache,* probably originating in Syria in the late first or early second century, adds: "If you do not have living [running] water, baptize in any other water; and if you cannot in cold, then in warm. If you have neither, then pour water on the head three times. . . . Before baptism the one who baptizes and the one who is baptized must fast . . ." (*Didache,* 7). The *Didache,* Justin Martyr, and Hippolytus make it clear that the common form of baptism in the early church was immersion. This symbolized dying and rising again with Christ. But immersion was not the only manner of baptism. Pictures from the Roman catacombs depict the initiate being drenched with water poured on him from a seashell. Cyprian, the bishop of Carthage in the middle of the third century, wrote that the method of sprinkling was also used. He went on to assert that the manner in which the water was applied was of minor importance as long as it was done by a priest of the true church. (*Letter* 69, 7—11)

The baptismal rite was preceded by a period of instruction.[4] During this period inquiry was made into motives, character, and occupation of the inquirer. No one living in adultery, no civil or military official of the state, no actor, gladiator, artist, or magician was instructed until these occupations were given up. Even individuals who had anything to do with the metal that went into the making of images were carefully checked. Extensive instructions were given in the Christian way of life as expounded in the life of our Lord and in the Sermon on the Mount.[5] Instruction in doctrine centered around the Trinity. Hippolytus reports that before a person under instruction, or a "catechumen," was admitted to baptism he was examined whether he "lived soberly," visited the sick, and otherwise showed a grasp of the Christian life. Catechumens who passed the scrutiny were daily "exorcised," that is, the evil spirit, in whose bondage they were

---

[4] The length of the period varied. Hippolytus indicates it usually took three years.

[5] See *Didache,* 1—3. (See also selection No. 1 in the Appendix.)

as pagans, was driven out of them as Jesus had driven the "unclean spirits" out of the "possessed" during His earthly ministry. The final exorcism was performed on Holy Saturday by the bishop, who laid his hand on the head of each candidate for it. Then he "sealed" his forehead, ears, and nose with the sign of the cross.

The baptism itself took place at "cockcrow" during Easter night. Each candidate was asked to renounce the devil and all his works. Then he was anointed with the "oil of exorcism" by a presbyter. After this, Hippolytus tells us, the candidate was led into the water, naked, and immersed three times by another presbyter. The elder or deacon asked him to testify to his belief in Father, Son, and Holy Spirit. The elder stated the affirmations of faith while the initiate simply affirmed his acceptance. The candidate usually did not recite the creed himself at this time.

After the newly baptized had emerged from the water, the "oil of thanksgiving" — symbolic of anointing an athlete — was applied to him, and he was brought into the congregation, where the bishop "laid his hands on him," anointed him for the third time — a participation in the royal anointing of Christ — and "signed" him on the forehead with the sign of the cross. It seems the "laying on of hands" was thought to be that part of the baptismal rite in which the Holy Spirit was poured out. The baptized was now allowed to join in the prayer, the offering, and the "holy kiss" of the congregation, and he received his first Communion, together with milk and honey, symbolizing his having entered the Promised Land.

Since baptism was the rite of receiving a new member into the church, the various parts of the ritual were meant to enhance its beauty and to establish its meaning in the memory. There is no evidence of a separate rite of confirmation in the first two centuries of the church.

Hippolytus specifically mentions that infants were baptized together with their parents. Other evidence makes it very clear that by the year 200 infant baptism was practiced in Rome, Carthage, and Alexandria, as well as in other sees.

It should be noted, however, that neither Justin Martyr nor the *Didache* mention infant baptism. The literature seems to assume it, just as the New Testament apparently does. When we are told in the Acts of the Apostles that "whole households" were baptized (16:15, 33), we can assume that, just as among the Jews in the baptism of their proselytes, this included the children.

The *Didache* asserts that no one was allowed to receive the Holy Communion unless he was baptized. In the section quoted above, Justin wrote that Christians were baptized because Christ said, "Unless you are born again you will not enter the kingdom of heaven." Contrasting the first birth as one of "necessity without our knowledge" with the second birth in baptism, Justin wrote, "We should not continue as children of necessity and ignorance but having knowledge obtain remission of sins." [6] He called baptism an "illumination" since "those learning these things are enlightened within."

THE CHRISTIAN SUNDAY

After describing baptism Justin continues: "On the day called Sunday meetings are held where the memoirs of the apostles and the writings of the prophets are read as long as time permits. After the reading is finished, the leader in a discourse invites us to imitate these things. Then we stand for prayer." (*1 Apology,* 67)

That *Sunday* was the normal day for common worship in the early church is confirmed by Pliny (110), governor extraordinary specifically appointed by the Emperor Trajan to keep order in Bithynia. He reported to Trajan that the Christians came together twice on this day. "They usually come together before daybreak and sing hymns back and forth to Christ as a god. They bind themselves by an oath not to commit crime but rather to avoid theft, robbery, and adultery. . . . Usually they come together somewhat later

---

[6] *1 Apology,* 61. In eastern communities the Feast of Epiphany was set aside to remember Christ's baptism.

to partake of food. . . ." [7] Christians celebrated the Eucharist
on Sunday because this was the day on which Jesus arose
from the dead. When they celebrated it, they were vividly
reminded that the Lord was indeed alive and, in keeping
with His promise, actually present in their midst. Each Sunday was a little Easter.

READINGS AND RESPONSE

The Sunday service included readings from the Old Testament, the "memoirs" of the apostles (most likely a reference
to the Gospels), the letters of Peter and Paul, and other materials. In the third century the Acts of the Apostles was read
in the period between Easter and Pentecost in some areas.
A great part of the material contained in what we call the
New Testament was shaped and preserved for and by use
in congregational worship.

Writings not included in the modern Bible, the letter of
Clement, for example, and that of Barnabas, as well as *The
Shepherd* of Hermas, were also read. These materials served
for instruction in Christian life just as the Bible does today.
The letter of Clement was written to the church in Corinth
encouraging them to Christian harmony and peace. In it
Clement reviewed many examples from the Old Testament
showing that God desires such concord. The letter that was
credited to Barnabas is actually a treatise on how to read
the Old Testament. It is filled with many interesting interpre-
tations but also points out that the Old Testament must be
read with its fulfillment in mind if it is to be properly understood. *The Shepherd* is a collection of visions, laws, and parables. Apparently written after a period of persecution, it encouraged stricter Christian discipline in the areas of charity
and chastity since God's grace was still available. Obviously
all of these could be profitably used for Christian instruction,
and they were.

Another type of literature that resulted in part from the

[7] Pliny the Younger, *Letter* X, xcvi.

worship of the early Christians was a combination of "historical romance" and preaching. Since many aspects of our Lord's life were not described in the Four Gospels, the faithful followers were eager for further information about Jesus — what He looked like, His childhood, added sayings, as well as what He did in hell. Accounts describing the details of Jesus' early life, such as *The Book of James* and the *Nativity of Mary,* were credited to eyewitnesses.[8] Answering the criticism of the pagans that Christianity was of humble origin, these writings stressed that Mary did not come from a poor village but was raised in Jerusalem as a "holy virgin" in the temple, that she was of royal descent, and that her parents were wealthy. When her parents died, Mary was supposedly placed with Joseph as his "betrothed" but actually to be kept as his daughter since Joseph was 80 years old and a widower. These and other details become "traditional" about Jesus' early life and background.

Luke also left many questions unanswered in his Acts of the Apostles. Peter's work as a missionary is described in part but then dropped to take up the activity of Paul. We are never told what happened to Peter. Luke tells the story of how Paul reached Rome without satisfying the curiosity of the reader about the later life of Paul. In 2 Cor. 11:23 ff. Paul makes mention of a number of events in his life that are never described in detail.

The curiosity of Christians about these matters was satisfied by biographies such as the *Acts of Peter* and the *Acts of Paul,* written anonymously but always credited to eyewitnesses, sometimes to an apostle writing in the first person. The *Acts of Peter* told how Peter, fleeing Rome, was met by Christ. When Christ asked, "Quo vadis?" ("Where are you going?") Peter knew that he was to return to the burning city and be crucified. In the *Acts of John* we learn that after John survived being boiled in oil he was exiled to Patmos. Later he became the leader of the church in Ephesus. Two

---

[8] These accounts are usually classified as "apocryphal literature." See any good encyclopedia under the term.

incidents from his life are especially descriptive. The first illustrates how much John detested heresy. "When John the disciple went into the bath at Ephesus, he saw Cerinthus [the Gnostic] inside. He rushed out crying, 'Flee, for surely the bath will fall with Cerinthus, the enemy of truth, inside.' " When he was dying and his disciples asked him for one last word of advice, he repeated the words he had often spoken, "Little children, love one another." It is impossible for the modern historian to determine exactly how much or how little of this material is accurate.

Someone in the congregation, usually the leader, commented on the readings. One of the oldest Christian sermons extant, incorrectly entitled *The Second Letter of Clement,* is actually a homily on Is. 54:1 that probably dates from the middle of the second century. The preacher tells the congregation that they were the "desolate" referred to by Isaiah, but that Jesus rescued men from their blindness and that they ought to "rejoice" in this fact. He begins, "Brothers, we ought to consider Jesus Christ as judge of all, just as we do God." The sermon continues by enjoining the Christians to live apart from the sinful world, warning them against sexual sins, and especially against attendance at public entertainment. It concludes by reminding them of their baptism and by encouraging them to repent "while we are in this world."

After the sermon the congregation united in prayers which show a marked Jewish influence. Since Justin mentions that the leader was allowed to pray freely, he indicates that set patterns of prayers were apparently also in use. The prayers were followed by the Eucharistic offering, in Justin's scheme.

He does not mention any hymnody, but Pliny speaks of Christians singing together antiphonally. A number of chants are found in the New Testament, and Paul mentions "psalms, hymns, and spiritual songs" (Eph. 5:19). One of our first Christian hymns was composed in the second century and is found at the close of Clement of Alexandria's *Christ the Tutor:*

> *Shepherd, with wisdom tending*
> *Lambs of the royal flock;*
> *Thy simple children bring*
> *In one, that they may sing*
> *In solemn lays*
> *Their hymn of praise*
> *With guileless lips to Christ, their King.*[9]

EUCHARIST

Members of the congregation exchanged the kiss of peace,[10] expressing reconciliation with one another (see Matt. 5:22-24), to mark the beginning of the Eucharist, that is, the "Thanksgiving," the joyful and thankful response to the Christ expressed in the celebration of the Lord's Supper. Justin describes it:

> After baptizing the person who has been instructed and has signified his assent, we lead him into the midst of the assembly of brethren. Then they pray together for themselves, for the one illuminated, and for all, that having learned the truth we be made worthy, that we do the commands and receive salvation. After prayers we exchange the kiss. Then bread and a cup of water mixed with wine are brought to the leader of the group. The leader takes them, praises the Father of the universe through the name of the Son and the Holy Spirit, and also offers thanksgiving at some length that we have been thought worthy to receive these things. The congregation answers with "Amen," which means "So be it" in Hebrew. After this the deacons distribute to each one present a portion of what is consecrated and also take it to those who are absent.
>
> We call this food "Eucharist." No one is allowed to partake unless he believes what we teach, has been baptized, and lives after the manner of Christ. We do not think that this is common bread and drink, but just as Jesus Christ our Savior took flesh and blood for our salvation, so this food, consecrated by the word of prayer . . . is the flesh and blood of that incarnate Jesus. The apostles in their memoirs, called Gospels, handed down what Jesus commanded them. . . . (*1 Apology,* 65)

---

[9] See H. M. Dexter's modern version of this hymn in *The Lutheran Hymnal* (St. Louis: Concordia Publishing House, 1941), No. 628.

[10] See Rom. 16:16; 1 Thess. 5:26; 2 Cor. 13:12; 1 Peter 5:14.

At this point Justin quotes the Words of Institution and then describes the distribution.

The earliest celebrations of the Eucharist took place in the setting of an actual meal. This meal is sometimes called the agape, or the love feast. St. Paul refers to a Communion celebration that was associated with a meal when he refuses to commend the Corinthians for making holy things common by gorging themselves and slighting the poor during the "Lord's Supper." He tells them that if they are that hungry they should eat at home (1 Cor. 11:18-22). In any case each individual brought food, the congregation partook of it together, rich and poor alike, and the rest was given to the poor. Ignatius (c. 110) referred to the celebration of agape feasts in Antioch, which still may have included the Eucharist. By the time of Justin Martyr (c. 150) the Eucharist seems to have been celebrated separately. He does not mention the two together. In Bithynia the Christians perhaps discontinued the feasts because these were considered suspicious by the authorities. In Corinth the separation may have occurred as a result of the abuses mentioned above. The date when various localities allowed this separation differs from place to place. The finest description of the agape separate from the Eucharist comes from the hand of Tertullian (c. 200), an elder in Carthage, in an Apology similar to Justin's:

> Much commotion is made about the modest upper room of the Christians. Our feast is explained by its name. . . . We benefit the needy with the good things of the feast. We are not like your parasites who satisfy their great cravings . . . but, as with God Himself, a genuine respect is shown for the lowly. . . . Before eating, the participants pray to God; in their conversation they remember that God is listening. . . . Each is requested to sing a song, either one from the Scriptures or one of his own making. As we begin with prayer we also close with prayer. (*Apology*, 39)

Remnants of the joint Eucharist-agape continued, however, when members of the congregation brought bread, wine, olives, and cheese, staples of the Mediterranean diet, to the altar during the offering, for distribution to the needy. Justin

writes: "Those who are willing to share part of their wealth
give as much as they desire. What is collected is deposited
with the leader, who takes care of widows, orphans, the sick,
prisoners, and travelers among us. We do this on Sunday
since it was on the first day of the week that God made the
universe and also that Jesus Christ our Savior rose from the
dead . . ." (*1 Apology,* 67). Only the baptized in good
standing were allowed to take part in this "oblation."

The celebration of the Lord's Supper gets the name
"Eucharist" from the prayer of thanksgiving that was said
over the offerings, as Justin suggests, "that we might give
thanks to God for creating everything for the sake of man,
for delivering us from the sin in which we were born, and
for destroying the dominions and powers through Him who
suffered." (*Dialogue with Trypho,* 14)

This prayer of thanksgiving was of central importance in
all of the early Christian liturgies. Its roots lie in Jewish
prayers of thanksgiving and in the "giving of thanks" associated with the supper that Jesus celebrated with His disciples
on the night He was betrayed. The earliest example is from
the *Didache:*

> This is how to give thanks. First in connection with the
> cup: "We thank You, our Father, for the holy vine of
> David, Your Child, which You have revealed through Jesus,
> Your Child. To You be glory forever."
> Then in connection with the piece [broken off the loaf]:
> "We thank You, our Father, for the life and knowledge
> which You have revealed through Jesus, Your Child. To
> You be glory forever. As this piece was scattered over
> the hills and then was brought together and made one, so
> let Your church be brought together from the ends of the
> earth into Your kingdom. For Yours is the glory and the
> power through Jesus Christ forever." [11]

Perhaps these prayers best express the richness and beauty
of early Christian liturgical expression. In *The Apostolic
Tradition* the prayer of thanksgiving emphasized the redeem-
ing activity of Jesus Christ, "who, fulfilling Thy will, and
winning for Himself a holy people, spread out His hands

---

[11] *Didache,* 9. See Richardson, p. 175.

when He came to suffer, that by His death He might set free them who believed on Thee. . . ." The Words of Institution, set within the Eucharistic prayer, are followed by: "Having in memory, therefore, His death and resurrection, we offer to Thee the bread and the cup, yielding Thee thanks. . . ." Finally there is a plea that the Holy Spirit be poured out on the congregation through the elements: "Send Thy Holy Spirit upon the offerings of Thy holy church; that Thou, gathering them into one, wouldst grant to all Thy saints who partake to be filled with [the] Holy Spirit. . . ." [12]

The wealth of liturgical material that remains from the celebration of the Eucharist by early Christians supports the thesis that the Eucharist was the most important element in their worship every Lord's Day. Certain liturgical responses such as "The Lord be (or "is") with you" and "And with thy spirit," along with the *Sursum corda,* "Lift up your hearts," are preserved in *The Apostolic Tradition* (200). These phrases illustrate the joyful and thankful character of the Eucharist. They remind us of the words from the Acts of the Apostles describing the Jerusalem church: "They partook of food with glad and generous hearts, praising God. . . ." (Acts 2:46, 47 RSV)

In the distribution leavened bread was used. The wine was mixed with water. The deacons took the elements to the worshipers. In addition, the newly baptized were given milk and honey to symbolize that they were babes in Christ but also to show that they were now in the Promised Land, the land "flowing with milk and honey."

Some of the early texts suggest that only the baptized in good standing were allowed to remain for the Eucharistic part of the liturgy. We do not know when this so-called *disciplina arcani* ("secret discipline") began, but it died out in the sixth century.

The Christians of this period were more concerned with worthy participation in the Eucharist than with verbalizing a doctrine about what was involved. We have Tertullian's

---

[12] *Apostolic Tradition,* I, iv, 4—13. See the edition by B. S. Easton (Cambridge: University Press, 1934).

treatise *On Baptism* from this period (c. 200) but we do not have a similar doctrinal account of Holy Communion. From many scattered references, including that above by Justin, it is obvious that the Christians believed they received Christ's body and blood in the Eucharist. Irenaeus puts it this way: "When the mixed cup and the bread that has been prepared receive the Word of God and become the Eucharist, the body and blood of Christ, and by these our flesh grows and is confirmed, how can they say that flesh cannot receive the free gift of God, which is eternal life, since it is nourished by the body and blood of the Lord and made a member of Him?" [13]

The body and blood are present with the bread and wine in the consecration: "The bread from the fruit of the earth is no longer merely bread when it receives the invocation. It is Eucharist, made up of two realities, the earthly and the heavenly. . . ." Ignatius of Antioch states this in stronger terms than Tertullian, who veers toward more symbolic terminology. But it is important to remember that the refinement of Eucharistic thought concerning the real presence resulting from medieval Scholastic thought and the debates of the 16th century is not found in these early fathers. They did not speculate. They accepted the miracle. That they received the Eucharist frequently is indicated by the fact that when a Christian missed the Sunday service a deacon automatically brought the Eucharist to his house.

The worship of the early church was not as fixed and formal as it was later to become. But it did not lack forms either. Many parts of the traditional liturgical framework are not found in the documents from this period. The Eucharistic liturgy contained no confession and absolution, and there is no explicit reference to the Kyrie, the Creed, or the Our Father. Prayers, hymns, and responses, slowly accumulated by the worshiping communities all over the world, give us the many ingredients of worship that are known in Christendom today.

---

[13] *Against Heresies,* IV, xviii; V, ii.

III. ORGANIZATION

ORIGIN

The administrative structure of the early church grew out of her "liturgy," which included not merely worship of God but also service to men in works of love (2 Cor. 9:12; Phil. 2:17, 30). Especially in the earliest years of the church's life there was no single preconceived plan of organization. The patterns differed from one region to another. Christians organized to overcome difficulties and to meet the challenges of their time. But there was an unmistakable trend toward uniformity. While patterns are vaguely discernible in the period when the literature of the New Testament was written, by 250 all the churches were ruled by a bishop, who was assisted by elders.

ELDERS

As a rule, the early churches were led by elders, or presbyters (from the Greek for "elders"), as were the Jewish synagogs. In the early literature, elders are often referred to as "overseers," or "bishops" in Greek. Paul, Luke, and Clement referred to the same group as elders in one sentence and bishops in the next.[1] Paul appointed elders in the churches he established.[2] Luke informs us that Paul and Barnabas were instructed by the church in Antioch to turn over to the elders in Jerusalem the moneys they had collected for the poor (Acts 11:30). A similar pattern was followed

---

[1] Acts 20:17, 28; Titus 1:5-7; *1 Clement,* 42—44.

[2] Acts 14:23. The pastoral office was thus a group ministry.

in the first decades of the second century in Alexandria, Philippi, Corinth, and Rome.

A primary function of the elders was to rule in the churches in the function of judges, that is, to maintain discipline; but they also engaged in teaching, as Paul indicates, "Let the elders who rule well be considered worthy of double honor, especially those who labor in preaching and teaching" (1 Tim. 5:17 RSV); and they had a key role in worship. Polycarp, a bishop of Smyrna in the first half of the second century, writing to the Philippian church, described the ideal Christian elder as a person "abstaining from all wrath, respect for persons, and unjust judgments; keeping away from all covetousness; not quickly crediting an evil report against anyone; not severe in judgment, knowing that we are all under the debt of sin" (*To the Philippians,* 6). Tertullian, a presbyter in Carthage at the end of the same century, reported his duties as a judge:

> In the same place [in worship] exhortations are made, rebukes and penalties are administered. The work of judging is carried on seriously among us since we know we are in the sight of God. Our judgments against those who have grievously sinned are a good example of the judgment that is to come. They are separated from our common prayers and our other sacred activities. The elders who preside over us are tried men with established character; the honor cannot be obtained through money. [An obvious reference to the fact that civil offices were usually purchased.] The things of God cannot be bought and sold. (*Apology,* 39)

When some of the elders in Corinth were removed from office by younger men, this caused strife in the congregation and a scandal among Christians all over the empire. The so-called *First Letter of Clement,* written in the name of the congregation in Rome to the church in Corinth in the year 96, was a reaction to this situation. The author of the letter, apparently a Roman presbyter-bishop named Clement, encouraged the Corinthians toward unity: "We are of the opinion . . . that those appointed by them [the disciples], or afterwards by other eminent men, with the consent of the whole church, and who have blamelessly served the cross of Christ

in a humble, disinterested, and peaceable spirit, and have
for a long time possessed the good opinion of all, cannot
justly be dismissed from the ministry. . . ." (*1 Clement*, 44)

Clement's letter indicates that the church in Corinth was
ruled by a *group* of *bishops*, or elders. He appears to use the
terms "bishop" and "presbyter" as synonyms (as Acts 20:
17 and 28 does). Since the term "bishop" in Greek means
"guardian" or "overseer," it may have been used *instead* of
"elder" in some areas. Clement suggests, and this is an important assumption, that elders have their office in succession
from Jesus Himself:

> The apostles received the Gospel for us from the Lord Jesus
> Christ; Jesus, the Christ, was sent from God. Thus Christ
> is from God and the apostles from Christ. In both cases
> the orderly procedure depends on God's will. And so the
> apostles . . . appointed their first converts, after testing them
> by the Spirit, to be bishops [note the plural] and deacons
> of future believers.[3]

Later on he adds:

> Thanks to the Lord Jesus Christ, our apostles saw that
> there would be fighting about the office of bishop. For this
> reason, having received accurate knowledge of the future,
> they appointed the officers mentioned by us. They also
> added a further testament which suggested that, should
> these die, other approved men should succeed to their
> ministry. In this light we feel that it is a breach of justice
> to remove men from office who have been appointed either
> by them or later on with the church's consent. . . . Your
> strife and rivalry, my brothers, touches matters of salvation.
> (*1 Clement*, 44, 45)

Clement based this understanding of ecclesiastical tradition
on injunctions attributed to our Lord, but also on a similar
order established by God in the Old Testament. Quoting
Isaiah, he wrote, "Nor was this any novelty, for the Scripture
had mentioned bishops and deacons long before. For this
is what Scripture says somewhere: 'I will appoint their
bishops in righteousness and their deacons in faith.' " [4] The

---

[3] *1 Clement*, 42. See Richardson, p. 62.

[4] Ibid., 42, quoting Is. 60:17 from memory or in an unknown Greek
version.

order in the Old Testament and the order established by Christ, argues Clement, demand that elders appointed in an orderly manner may not be deposed.

In some areas congregations perhaps had the services of "prophets" and "teachers" available but not those of "elders." The work of prophets in New Testament times is not entirely clear. Some of them were able to foretell the future (Acts 11:27), others were endowed with the special ability to interpret the Old Testament prophets reliably (1 Cor. 14:1-5). When a prophet was available, he apparently led the celebration of the Eucharist. The *Didache* may have been written to such an area — probably somewhere in Syria. The specific concern of the Didachist was to help the churches avoid the difficulties connected with an *itinerant* ministry by distinguishing between false and true prophets on the basis of their ethical behavior and by electing permanent local officers. Many self-styled "prophets" moved from place to place and exploited the Christian communities. This was possible because of a practice taken over from the Jewish synagog, the mother of the Christian church, which allowed anyone, including strangers, to speak in the services.[5] Besides, the early Christians were mindful of the Scriptural injunction, "Quench not the Spirit" (1 Thess. 5:19). The Didachist urged, "You must elect for yourselves bishops [note the plural] and deacons. . . . For their ministry to you is identical with that of the prophets and teachers" (*Didache,* 15). They should therefore be given an honor equal to that of the prophets.

BISHOPS

The most important organizational development in the second century, indeed in the whole of early Christian history, is the emergence of a bishop who exercised his powers distinct but not separate from the elders. However, a bishop in the second century was a pastor of a congregation rather than an individual set over a larger area. By the third cen-

---

5 Luke 4:17ff.; Acts 13:15; 14:1.

tury he is often referred to as "father," or papas (from which the word "pope") in Greek.

The origins of the single bishop, as distinct from the other elders, are obscure. It seems that in the course of time the ministry of the presiding elder developed into a separate office and that it was given a monopoly on the title of "bishop." It is also entirely possible that some congregations had such a "monarchical" bishop from the beginning. There were early Christians who believed that this office could be traced back to the time of the apostles. Clement, a teacher in Alexandria c. 200, suggested that the disciple John in Ephesus appointed such bishops. It was commonly believed that Peter was in Rome and established this office there. James the brother of our Lord was considered the first bishop in Jerusalem.

This undeniable trend toward the authority of one bishop in the congregation is clearly underscored by the letters of Ignatius, who suggested that the Holy Eucharist, Baptism, and even the agape would not accomplish their purpose without his consent. Ignatius was a bishop in Antioch at the beginning of the second century. We have seven letters from his hand written on the way to martyrdom in Rome. As he journeyed from Antioch to Rome, taking the land route through Asia Minor (probably the same roads that St. Paul traveled), he wrote letters to various congregations in that area where he heard that heresy was threatening. It is in this connection that he, claiming to be inspired by the Holy Spirit, suggested that if anyone was separated from the bishop he was no longer in the church:

> Flee from schism as the source of mischief. You should all follow the bishop as Jesus Christ did the Father. Follow too the presbytery as you would the apostles; and respect the deacons as you would God's Law. Nobody must do anything that has to do with the church without the bishop's approval. You should regard that Eucharist as valid which is celebrated either by the bishop or by someone he authorizes. Where the bishop is present, there let the congregation gather, just as where Jesus Christ is, there is the Catholic Church. [This is the first time the term *Catholic*

Church is used in early Christian literature.] Without the
bishop's supervision, no baptisms or agapes are permitted.
On the other hand, whatever he approves pleases God as
well.[6]

Ignatius assumed that the bishop was always in agreement
with his presbyters before he acted, the presbyters acting
as his council.

Ignatius had no theory of succession such as is found
in his contemporary, Clement of Rome. He suggested that
the bishop represents God in the Christian community, the
presbyters represent the apostles, and the deacons, who
serve the will of the bishop, represent Christ the "Servant." [7]
As the will of God among men was in the hands of the
apostles and carried out by Christ, so in the congregation
the will of the bishop is in the hands of the presbyters and
carried out by the deacons. If Ignatius had been asked why
this order existed he probably would have answered that
God ordained it. It was not Ignatius' purpose, however,
to enhance the office of bishop for its own sake; he was
interested rather in preserving the unity of the church in
the face of schism and true teaching in the face of Gnostic
heresy (see pp. 54—57). He felt that giving one man
greater authority was the best way to preserve unity and
orthodoxy. It is a matter of historical record that the bishops
did play an important role in curbing heresy.

By the first decades of the third century all the churches
had a bishop in control of their affairs. Cyprian, bishop in
Carthage until his martyrdom in 258, gives us the best insight into the powers that accumulated to the office of bishop.
He claimed that the bishop was a divinely appointed high
priest to mediate between God and the people. This is called
"sacerdotalism." The Old Testament distinction between the
priesthood and the people was an important influence here.
It was only by the bishop's hand that members could be
admitted into the church, that officers could assume their
duties in the congregation, or that other clergymen could

---

[6] *Smyrneans,* 8. See Richardson, p. 115.

[7] The Greek *diakonos* means servant.

be ordained. Cyprian emphasized that each bishop had these powers in his own right by divine authority through his standing in the apostolic succession. Only a bishop ordained by another bishop in good standing could confer the special spiritual gift which belonged to the members and officials of the church. Cyprian likewise insisted that excommunication was in his jurisdiction alone and that there was no forgiveness of gross sins apart from the bishop.

OTHER MINISTRIES

A form of the multiple ministry persisted in the clergy who assisted the bishop in carrying out the work of the ministry. A good description of these offices is found in *The Apostolic Tradition* (c. 200) of Hippolytus (I, 9—15). Deacons brought the Eucharistic offerings of the faithful to the bishop, carried the consecrated bread and wine to the communicants, distributed alms to the poor, and cared for the sick and dying (there were no hospitals) under the direction of the bishop. In larger congregations subdeacons were appointed to assist the deacons especially in informing the bishop of cases of sickness. Deacons received further help from the acolytes, who carried letters, distributed alms, and ministered to those in prison, and from the doorkeepers, who provided for cleaning and lighting the place of worship and for the burial of Christian martyrs. Widows and virgins were especially designated to spend much time in prayer and to assist the deacons by helping the sick and the poor women. Exorcists also helped the deacons by caring for those deranged by evil spirits, especially among the sick. Additional officers included confessors, individuals who had confessed the faith before the authorities and suffered in persecution, and readers, those especially gifted with the ability to read the Scripture lessons well.

THE PRIESTHOOD OF ALL

Along with the suggestion that believers ought not hanker after the office of bishop, Clement of Rome affirmed that

"Unto the high priest his proper services have been entrusted.
. . . The layman is bound by the layman's code." This is
the first time the word "layman" occurs in Christian literature. Of the layman he asserted, "We ought not transgress
the regulations put down for our service but do it in reverence" (*1 Clement*, 40, 41). Although Clement recognized
the distinction between clergy and laity, he also believed
that the laity had a priestly ministry. This was evidenced
in the liturgy when each Christian in good standing participated in the Eucharistic offering.

As the evidence of an excessive emphasis on the sacer-
dotal structure accumulated, voices of protest were raised,
Tertullian's among them. Tertullian's individualism ultimately led him to break with the congregation in Carthage,
not because of any doctrinal disagreement primarily, but
because he believed too many Christians were not practicing
what they preached. Discipline was at a low ebb, he thought.
When he disagreed with his bishop, he insisted that it didn't
matter since the church existed wherever two or three were
gathered together in the name of Jesus Christ. This was not a
popular belief in 200 any longer, since Ignatius' emphasis
that the church existed where the bishop was had become
rather common. Tertullian stands out as one who defended
the thesis that all Christians have a ministry that Christ
established: "Are not laymen priests also? It is written, 'He
hath made us kings and priests.' Only the authority of the
church has made this difference between clergy and laity.
If there are no clergy around, you offer [the eucharist], you
baptize, you are a priest for yourself. And even though you
are only laymen, when there are three of you together you are
church. Each of us stands before God on the basis of his
faith and nothing else." (*Exhortation to Chastity*, 7)

There are other indications also that laymen played an
important role. Justin Martyr, a teacher in Rome and elsewhere, stands out as an important theologian of the second
century, even though he had no regular office in the church,
being at most a lay preacher. The greatest theologian of
this period, Origen of Alexandria, began his teaching career

as a layman. Indeed, it has been said that the great teachers in the early church were seldom the bishops, although there are a few examples of bishops who were also great teachers. The laity also had a voice in the selection of the clergy which was to care for them. The bishop of a local parish was elected by the local elders with the consent of the congregation, or by the congregation itself with the approval of other bishops in the area.[8] Cyprian thought of this as an apostolic regulation. This custom persisted in Rome, Milan, Carthage, and probably also in the East, as is suggested by the participation of the people in the election of Chrysostom to the See of Constantinople in the late fourth century.

ECCLESIASTICAL ORGANIZATION ON A WIDER BASIS

The early sources reveal very little of anything analogous to modern supracongregational organizations; each congregation was an autonomous unit. There was of course communication between various churches but no administrative unity. However, when a city congregation became too large, it split into two or more churches headed by elders but remaining under the rule of the original bishop. The rural churches around the city were likewise under the bishop's spiritual jurisdiction.

A development away from local autonomy became inevitable and imperative as soon as inter- and intracongregational strife occurred and schism threatened. The emergence of factions ready to name their own bishops, of heresy, and of differences in dealing with gross sins necessitated the use of arbiters from the outside to adjudicate difficulties. The matter of uniformity in observing the Feast of the Resurrection was another problem requiring decisions above the local level. Generally Easter was celebrated on the same day of the week, Sunday, the day of the resurrection.[9] In part of the church, however, Easter was celebrated in accordance with the Jewish Passover observance on a particular day of the

---

[8] *1 Clement,* 44. See also Hippolytus, I, 1—3.

[9] Easter was *the* important feast day in the early church. Epiphany, celebrated as the remembrance of our Lord's baptism, was also important in the East. Christmas was instituted only later.

month, the 14th of *Nisan,* regardless of the day of the week. Such disunity was considered scandalous. Gnostic and Montanist (see pp. 54—56) assertions that they represented authentic Christianity, especially their claims to knowledge or revelation not accessible to all believers, also caused division in the churches. For the adjudication of such larger problems bishops of various cities in a geographical area began to meet in conferences, or councils, as they came to be called.

In the course of the second century the bishops of provincial capitals, or metropolises, in the East, following the pattern of imperial administration, acquired jurisdiction over the bishops of the towns within their provinces. They received the status of "metropolitans." In the West the jurisdiction of the "metropolitan" developed only later. Bishops, however, never settled issues in a dictatorial manner but through council. At first such councils were gatherings of all the bishops in a given area, together with their presbyters, deacons, and some laymen. A council to represent the *whole* church, that is, a universal (or ecumenical) council, was not known until 325, the time of the First Council at Nicaea in Asia Minor.

With the rapid expansion of the church and a growing number of problems the tendency developed to look to some individual with final authority. Before the fourth century the Roman church was honored as the place where Peter and Paul worked and died, but it had no power of judgment recognized by the church as a whole. However, a third-century Roman bishop did claim to be *the* guardian of the true tradition, and Victor, the bishop of Rome (198), excommunicated those who did not agree with his position on the dating of Easter. A heathen Roman emperor, Aurelian (c. 270), suggested that church disputes might be settled by turning them over to the judgment of Rome. But no Roman bishop in this early period claimed to have any jurisdiction outside of his province because of some authority derived from Peter. This is a later development.

Indeed, there were many indications that the Roman bishop

was rebuked whenever he interfered in the activities of other bishops. When Victor attempted to force all of the churches to conform to Rome's dating in the celebration of Easter, Irenaeus reminded him that this was not the manner in which such difficulties were settled. Tertullian rebuked Callistus, bishop of Rome in the years after Victor, for "immodesty" when he claimed to have certain exclusive powers from Peter to remit sins. Even Cyprian, who held that Jesus Himself made Peter a symbol of ecclesiastical unity by giving the keys to him individually, did not acknowledge the right of Rome to interfere in other areas to keep ecclesiastical peace. Cyprian also had no qualms about accusing bishop Stephen, his counterpart in Rome, of improper and unapostolic practice in not rebaptizing converts to the Roman church from a heretical group. Firmilian, a bishop in Cappadocia, called Stephen a "Judas" in the church for this practice.[10]

The Roman church was highly honored in the early church, but this does not change the fact that organizationally this church had no more right to interfere in the affairs of another church than any other bishop in Christendom. *Each* was to be responsible for all. This was the position of Irenaeus, Tertullian, Cyprian, and perhaps, when all is said and done, also of Rome.

The New Testament concept of the church as *una sancta* [11] continued to have a strong influence on the thinking of the early church. This unity among the various churches in Christendom was assumed, however, rather than organized. There was no administrative structure to which one could point in order to show "unity." It was taken for granted that all except the heretics believed the same things and that they were doing the same work. They communicated with each other when difficulties arose; individuals traveled from one church to another as teachers; but there was no organization beyond this.

---

[10] The Council of Nicaea in 325, however, sided with Rome.

[11] Meaning "one and holy." Note the words of the Nicene Creed, "I believe in one holy catholic [Christian] and apostolic church." See Eph. 4:4-6; 5:27.

If there was any visible symbol of unity it was epitomized in the figure of the bishop associated with other bishops. Cyprian in his conference essay *On the Unity of the Catholic Church* insisted that there is only one church. This church is found where the bishop is. Ignatius had said this earlier, but he was speaking about the individual congregation. Cyprian applied this to the church at large. That is, he said that a group can call itself "church" only if it has a bishop who has been properly ordained and who is in unity with the other bishops of the church. There is, therefore, only one church. All who were not part of this empirical reality were not considered church. Cyprian allowed that they were at most "dead branches." He compared this church to Noah's ark, outside of which no one could be saved:

> It is especially necessary for us who preside in the church as bishops firmly to uphold unity. . . . The episcopate is one whole. Each bishop rules knowing he is responsible for the whole church. The church is one though she spreads over the whole world increasingly. She is the one sun with many rays and yet one light, or a tree with many branches but one base. Many streams that flow from one spring seem to be disconnected, but have one source. You cannot divide the light from the sun. The branch broken from the tree will not bud. The stream cut off from the spring dries up. So the unity of the one church all over the world cannot be broken. . . . She is spread all over but there is one head, one source, one mother boundlessly fruitful. Of her womb we are born, nourished by her milk, made alive by her breath.[12]

---

[12] *On the Unity of the Catholic Church,* 5. See also *Letter* 69, 2.

IV. TEACHING

APOSTOLIC TRADITION

Many bishops and teachers in the early church were the students of the apostles. In the early second century the bishop of Hierapolis in Asia Minor, a certain Papias, had been a hearer of a disciple of the apostle John. Polycarp, who later became bishop of Smyrna, was a pupil of John himself. This Polycarp was in turn the teacher of Irenaeus (170), the bishop of the congregation in Lyons in Gaul. Irenaeus wrote about the hours he spent listening to Polycarp reminisce about John:

> I recall the events of those years better than those of recent time . . . so that I can recall the very place where the blessed Polycarp sat and discoursed, his goings in and out, the character of his life and his appearance, the lessons he gave to the public. He would tell of his conversations with John and the others who knew the Lord. He would recite their words from memory, especially what they told him about the Lord. Polycarp repeated what he heard from these eyewitnesses about His words and works, always in accord with the Scriptures. I used to listen very carefully noting everything in my heart rather than on paper. Again and again these memorized words go through my mind.[1]

In this way the teachings of the apostles were passed down by word of mouth from generation to generation. This "handing down" was called "tradition." When Irenaeus debated with the Gnostics about who was teaching the apostolic doctrine, he pointed to his clear relationship to John. He insisted, furthermore, that there was such a tradition of apostolic teaching in other churches:

---

[1] Eusebius, *Ecclesiastical History,* V, xx, 4.

The tradition of the apostles, made clear in all the world, can be clearly seen in every church by those who wish to behold the truth. We can enumerate those who were established by the apostles as bishops in the churches, and their successors down to our own time. . . . They certainly wished those whom they were leaving as their successors, handing over to them their own teaching position, to be perfect and irreproachable, since their sound conduct would be of great benefit [to the church], and failure on their part the greatest calamity.[2]

Early Christian teachers pointed not only to oral tradition but also to the fact that the writings of the apostles existed in the same churches that they had established. These writings were called the written tradition. They contained the same teaching that had been handed down orally. Tertullian (195) told the heretics who opposed him to check these originals: "Come now . . . run through the apostolic churches, where the chairs of the apostles still preside over their areas, where the authentic letters of the apostles are still read aloud. . . . If Achaea is nearest to you, you have Corinth. If you are not far from Macedonia, you have Philippi and Thessalonica. . . ." [3] The writings of the apostles were called "Scripture" and were honored together with the Old Testament as the Word of God Himself.

"Scripture" referred, however, first of all, to the Old Testament. In the period under our survey the books which Protestants call "Apocrypha" were quoted as part of the Old Testament. These are books which, originating in Jewish communities outside Palestine, especially in Alexandria, were probably not in the Old Testament used by the Jews in Palestine, where Hebrew was still studied. Most of them were written in Greek and included in the Septuagint, a Greek translation of the Old Testament from the second or third century B. C., also originating in Egypt. The Old Testament in this Greek form was read in worship.

Various apostolic "memoirs" of Christ were also read in worship. Gospel accounts other than our traditional four

---

[2] *Against Heresies,* III, iii, 1. See Richardson, pp. 371, 372.
[3] *Proscription of Heretics,* 36.

(such as *The Gospel of the Hebrews*) were circulated, but by the year 200 only our four were commonly read in worship. Irenaeus described the Gospel accounts he knew:

> They [the disciples] first preached it abroad, and then later by the will of God handed it down to us in Writings, to be the foundations and pillar of our faith. For it is not right to say that they preached before they came to perfect knowledge, as some dare to say, boasting that they are the correctors of the apostles. For after our Lord had risen from the dead, and they were clothed with the power from on high when the Holy Spirit came upon them, they were filled with all things and had perfect knowledge. . . . So Matthew among the Hebrews issued a writing of the Gospel in their own tongue, while Peter and Paul were preaching in Rome and founding the church. After their decease Mark, the disciple and interpreter of Peter, also handed down to us in writing what Peter had preached. Then Luke, the follower of Paul, recorded in a book the Gospel as it was preached by him. Finally John, the disciple of the Lord, who had also lain on His breast, himself published the Gospel, while he was residing at Ephesus in Asia. . . . If anyone does not agree with these, he despises the companions of the Lord. . . .[4]

Various other writings, such as letters of the apostles and "Acts" describing their ministry, were also read in services (see pp. 33—34). Little concern is evident at first to limit the variety of these readings; it was only by the middle of the fourth century that there was almost universal agreement on what books were part of the New Testament.

It was as a result of conflict with the claims of Montanist and Gnostic heresies that the church fathers, the classical writers and teachers of the early church, came to grips with the question of exactly what formed the legitimate basis of teaching.

Montanism spread from Asia Minor (c. 150) with the claim that it possessed revelation from the Holy Spirit demanding purer ethical conduct and separation from communities of Christians less pure.

There were many types of *Gnosticism*. Essentially Gnos-

---

[4] *Against Heresies,* III, i, 1. See Richardson, p. 370.

tics reacted negatively to the natural world in which they lived, claiming that it was the product of an evil demon. The ideal world is above all this. To reach this ideal world the soul must be enlightened by a savior sent from the true God to ignite a spark that exists in certain selected individuals by giving them an experience *(gnosis)* of heavenly reality. Since the physical creation is evil, this savior cannot be "man" in any natural sense. For this reason the Docetists (from the Greek *dokeo,* "to seem"), early Christians who claimed that Jesus only *seemed* to be human, are sometimes classified as Gnostics. But because of the number and variety of the dualistic groups, Docetists were not necessarily Gnostics. Disdaining material creation, a Gnostic either abstained from sexual relationships or engaged in every debauchery because he believed the body irrelevant to the life of the spirit.

An extensive cache of Gnostic writings was found in 1945 at Nag-Hammadi in Egypt, giving us in hitherto unknown quantities firsthand evidence of what the Gnostics wrote. Such writings as *The Gospel of Truth* and the *Gospel of Thomas* were among the important finds. This discovery is easily as important for the study of early Christianity as the Dead Sea Scrolls.

Gnostics who claimed to be Christians were marked by their rejection of the God of the Old Testament. These Gnostics claimed that the God whom Jesus Christ called His "Father" was not the God who was described in the Old Testament. Marcion, the son of a Christian bishop in Pontus, traveled to Rome before the middle of the second century and expounded this new theology there. In a writing called the *Antitheses* he contrasted the God acting in the O. T. with Jesus' description of His Father. The contrasts revolved around the claim that in the Old Testament God (Yahweh) is "just," a God of the Law; while the God described by Jesus is "loving," the God of the Gospel. Though Marcion had perhaps the deepest appreciation of God's free grace in Jesus Christ of anyone in his day, he stressed "justification by grace" to the point of denying that a loving God could at the same time be just. He found it necessary in support of his thesis to "use the scissors," as Tertullian wrote, on those parts of the New Testament that were not compatible with his thinking. Having rejected the Old Testament as irrelevant for the Christian religion, Marcion accepted the Gospel of Luke and Paul's letters, but only after he had cut out those sections where either Jesus or Paul referred to Yahweh as God.

Gnostics claimed that their writings were the authoritative interpretation of what Jesus really meant to say. They claimed to have a "secret tradition" passed down from Peter and Paul — a tradition they could not establish and also one that no one else ever heard of — that confirmed their "Gospel." The Christian fathers pointed to the churches that the apostles established, emphasizing that if there were any "secret" doctrine the disciples surely would have imparted it to the shepherds they appointed over their congregations. Irenaeus and Tertullian also pointed to the accepted writings of the apostles, showing how they disagreed with the teachings of the Gnostics. This conflict was very important because it forced Christians to recognize more precisely which of the writings used in the church were actually apostolic and authoritative.

The teachings of the apostles, passed down orally and in their writings, were summarized in the Rules of Faith. These Rules, like creeds, verbalized in brief form what was taught by the church all over the world. Unlike creeds, however, these summaries were not used in the eucharistic liturgy nor composed specifically to condemn heretical positions, but were, rather, summaries of what was taught to the catechumens entering the church. These Rules also differed from the later universal creeds in that they were not recited in precisely the same way, with exactly the same words, in every area of the church. It is possible to read the Rule in Irenaeus, Tertullian, and Origen; but the words are nowhere alike. We quote Irenaeus' as an example:

> Now the church, although scattered over the whole civilized world to the end of the earth, received from the

apostles and their disciples its faith in one God, the Father Almighty, who made the heaven, and the earth, and the seas, and all that is in them, and in one Christ Jesus, the Son of God, who was made flesh for our salvation, and in the Holy Spirit, who through the prophets proclaimed the dispensations of God — the comings, the birth of a virgin, the suffering, the resurrection from the dead, and the bodily reception into the heavens of the Beloved, Christ Jesus our Lord, and His coming from the heavens in the glory of the Father to restore all things, and to raise up all flesh, that is, the whole human race, so that every knee may bow, of things in heaven, and on earth, and under the earth, to Christ Jesus our Lord and God and Savior and King, according to the pleasure of the invisible Father, and every tongue may confess Him, and that He may execute righteous judgment on all. The spiritual powers of wickedness, and the angels who transgressed and fell into apostasy, and the godless, and wicked, and lawless, and blasphemers among men He will send to eternal fire. But to the righteous and holy, and those who have kept His commandments and have remained in His love, some from the beginning (of life) and some since their repentance, he will by His grace give life incorrupt, and will clothe them with eternal life.[5]

This was the message of the early church. It was called the Apostolic Rule since the fathers believed that it summarized the teaching handed down from the apostles. Any new teaching was measured by this Rule.

JESUS, MESSIAH AND SAVIOR

The major emphasis in the theology of the early church was that Jesus Christ is the Savior from sin and death. In the Acts of the Apostles the sermons of Peter and Paul illustrate the centrality of "Jesus is the Christ" in the message of earliest Christianity, "Let all the house of Israel therefore know assuredly that God has made this Jesus whom you crucified both Lord and Christ" (Acts 2:36). As various controversies beset the church and as Christians attempted to communicate their faith to others, this message of salvation too often took a seemingly secondary position. The Gospel does not shine through with the same brilliance in

---

[5] *Against Heresies*, I, x, 1. See Richardson, p. 360.

Clement of Rome as it does in Paul even though they were writing to the same congregation with many of the same problems. The apologists in the second century were more concerned to defend the Christian belief in one God than they were to impress the message of salvation. In some of the Apologies the saving Word of Jesus Christ is hardly discussed. This was certainly unusual, but the fact that it happened illustrates the point. On the other hand these instances must be weighed against other evidence which indicates that the message "Jesus is Savior" did remain central.

This centrality is illustrated by the writings of Irenaeus (c. 200), bishop of Lyons in southern Gaul. In his works *Demonstration of Apostolic Preaching* and *Against Heresies* he presented a brilliant interpretation of the Atonement, in which the centrality of Jesus Christ both in history and in the individual relationship between God and man is obvious. His view is summarized in the word "recapitulation," or "summing up." The Greek word for it, which can also mean "uniting," was used by Paul when he wrote, "For He has made known to us in all wisdom and insight the mystery of His will, according to His purpose which He set forth in Jesus Christ as a plan for the fullness of time, *to unite* all things in Him" (Eph. 1:10 RSV). Irenaeus taught that Jesus summed up in Himself the entire history of mankind — as all men are in Adam by birth, they are in Christ by rebirth. Christ is the Head of God's new creation, the church. It is God's purpose ultimately to unite all men under Christ.

When God created Adam "in His image," according to Irenaeus, God meant that man, unlike the animals and angels, was to contemplate His glory and goodness. But God did not create Adam with the fully developed ability to do this. Only Christ is fully the Image of God. Adam was created to develop "into the fullness of the image." Genesis does not record that Adam was "the image" but rather that he was made "in the image." In Paradise, therefore, Adam was not fully developed spiritually. Irenaeus did not mean to say that Adam was imperfect, but rather that he was innocent like a child, not knowing the difference between good and evil.

Irenaeus felt that the devil took advantage of Adam's innocence just as an adult can take advantage of a child. God planned that Adam should ultimately be "like God." But the devil interrupted this spiritual development by tempting Adam to presumption — the presumption of being "like God" and of "knowing good and evil" without spiritual struggle. Adam's disobedience meant that he turned his thoughts in upon himself instead of continuing in the contemplation of God. No longer able to grow in the knowledge of God, Adam was cast out of Paradise. Repeating the phrase of Paul, "In Adam all die" (1 Cor. 15:22), Irenaeus discussed Adam as a historical figure but also as the representative of mankind.

In order to rescue mankind from this plight, Christ "the Image," became a man and recapitulated all that man experiences: childhood, manhood, temptation, and death. But there is one important difference. Christ reversed what happened to man. Man's life is one of defeat by evil forces. When Christ became a man, He was not defeated by evil but gained the victory over it because of His perfect obedience to the will of God. The history of the first Adam recorded in Genesis is reversed by the story of the second Adam in the Gospel (1 Cor. 15:22; Rom. 5:17-21). Irenaeus wrote: "He has therefore, in His work of recapitulation, summed up all things, both waging war against our enemy and crushing him who at the beginning had led us away captive in Adam . . . in order that as our species went down to death through a vanquished man, so we may ascend to life again through a victorious One." [6]

Irenaeus also discussed the temptation of Christ as part of this recapitulation. The devil took Jesus to a high mountain and tempted Him to be like God just as Adam had been tempted. But unlike Adam, Jesus was not a spiritual

---

[6] *Against Heresies*, V, xxi, 1.

infant; He was fully developed spiritually. Indeed, He was "the Image." Where Adam was disobedient to God's plan for his spiritual growth, Jesus reversed this by obediently answering the devil, "You shall worship the Lord your God, and Him only. . . ." (Luke 4:8 RSV)

Finally Jesus also experienced death. But he experienced it voluntarily in order to go the whole way with man. Here is where the reversal of the human situation really comes through. Since our Lord experienced death because He was perfectly obedient rather than disobedient, death could not hold Him. He victoriously triumphed over death. Irenaeus carefully analyzed the nature of the atonement that was simply stated by the writer to the Hebrews: "Since therefore the children share in flesh and blood, He Himself likewise partook of the same nature, that through death He might destroy him who has the power of death, that is, the devil." [7]

Jesus was then all that man was. But because He was also "the Image" of God, divine in every sense of the term, He did not succumb to temptation but was victorious over it. This began a new era for man. We divide history into B. C. and A. D. to illustrate in part that whereas "in Adam all died," in Christ "all are made alive." For Irenaeus these "alive" people made up the church. Entering the church through Baptism, each individual is incorporated into Christ and is thus restored to his original innocence and allowed once again to grow "into the fullness of the image of God in Christ." [8]

MONOTHEISM AND TRINITY

Early Christianity faced a polytheistic society, not a secular society. Gods abounded. All the Christian teachers who wrote "apologies" for Christianity to engage the pagan mind emphasized that Christianity taught monotheism. The Christians pointed to the teaching of Greek philosophy that there

---

[7] Heb. 2:14 RSV. See also Col. 2:15 and 1 John 3:8.
[8] See Eph. 4:11-13; Col. 1:15-20.

was only one source of being; that changelessness is one and simple rather than multiple and complex like the changeable. The Christians rehearsed the Epicurean criticisms of the traditional myths about the gods, adding their invective to the scoffing already common and echoing the Old Testament emphasis that "God is one." (Athenagoras, *Plea,* 5—8)

But it was not this simple. Christians also taught that Jesus was the Son of God. For this reason pagans and Jews insisted that Christianity was in fact the true polytheism. It was necessary, therefore, for Christians to show just how Jesus was related to the Father in order to substantiate their claims to monotheism. Apart from Gnosticism and Montanism, the other heresies in the early church arose from the attempts to describe this relationship. There were certain aspects about which all agreed. The general Christian practice was to baptize in the name of the Father, Son, and Spirit. Still they insisted that there was only one God. They taught that Jesus was the Savior of men and therefore had to be divine. But assuming all this, how is the relationship of the Godhead to Jesus Christ described? This was perhaps the most perplexing question that Christians faced in this early period. It did not receive an official solution until 451.

One of the first solutions to be offered was that by Justin Martyr. He was a philosopher turned Christian who worked with the *logos* idea as described in the Gospel of John: "In the beginning was the Word *(logos),* and the Word was with God, and the Word was God." He taught that this *logos* was "generated" — a word meaning "to come out of" as a branch comes out of a tree — out of the Father before time began. This generation, he said, did not involve any diminution of the essence of the Father nor was there any division that took place. He compared the relationship to that of the sun to its rays; the one comes out of the other but the rays never decrease the light of the sun. When he debated with Trypho, a Jew, about the meaning of the Old Testament he suggested that the many divine appearances in the Old Testament to the patriarchs were not by angels but rather by this "other divine being" the *logos*.[9] Justin was able to preserve the identity of the *logos* as well as its relationship to the Father, but the fact that he spoke of it as the "other" divine being disturbed many Christians.

In fear of constructions like Justin's, the "Monarchians" opposed this "logos speculation," as they called it, with an emphasis on the oneness of God (monarch-ians). So Praxeas, a teacher in Rome c. 190, taught that the Son was a mere "mode" or "form" that the Father became for a space of years in order to redeem man, only to discard it when the work was finished. Praxeas denied the essential "threeness" of God by insisting that there was no Father when there was a Son, and conversely, there was no Son either in the period before the Incarnation or after the Ascension — only the Father. This forced him into the position, as Tertullian suggested, of "crucifying the Father." Since the Gospels clearly state that it was the Son who died, and that the Son had a relationship to His Father, Praxeas' solution was not accepted.

Paul of Samosata, bishop of Antioch c. 270, is the classical example of another type of monarchianism. He taught that since God cannot change He certainly could not become a man. Paul explained what happened in Jesus by insisting that He was born and grew up as any other individual, but was later selected by God to become the Christ at His baptism when the voice spoke from heaven "This is My beloved Son. . . ." In these words God poured out on Jesus a special "power" to remain perfect and "adopted" Him to be the "firstborn" of God's new creation — the church. Paul preserved the oneness of God with this solution, but in the process made Jesus little more than a unique man.

Both Praxeas and Paul of Samosata were excommunicated by local councils. But their errors forced the church to develop refutations on the basis of the apostolic writings. The answers given in this period were not adequate, but

---

[9] *Dialogue with Trypho,* 55 ff. See Gen. 32:28; 18:1-8, 16-21.

they evidence a concern to be loyal to the apostolic witness. It is also true that sometimes the answers of this period are inadequate specifically because they were attempting to be loyal to the Scriptures. Sayings of our Lord such as "I and the Father are one" and "the Father is greater than I" posed a problem of interpretation especially since the verses of Scriptures were read in isolation rather than in larger sections.

In addition to the Scriptural approach, the fathers also attempted to give their answers a systematic or logical cast. This involved the church in the philosophical thought patterns of their time. Christians used words, for example, not just from the Bible but also from the philosophical classroom to express what they wanted to say. There was little concern to give formal logical expression to questions relating to the Godhead by the writers of the New Testament or even by the earliest Christian writers not included in the New Testament. They simply state certain basic, but unsystematized, facts about Jesus and the Father. Ignatius, for example, wrote that Jesus was "flesh yet spiritual, born yet unborn, God incarnate, true life in true death, sprung from Mary but also from God, subject to suffering and later beyond it" (*To the Ephesians,* 7). These statements were made but not explained. The first fathers to answer the Monarchians by trying to explain the true relationship between the Father and the Son were Tertullian in Carthage and Origen in Alexandria.

Tertullian's treatise *Against Praxeas* was the first attempt to systematize the church's understanding of the apostolic witness. He suggested that there is only one God (one monarch), one divine "substance," but that the one God consisted of three "persons." The word "person" is from the Latin word *persona* which originally meant a mask worn by an actor, then the role portrayed by the actor, and finally an individual. By speaking of three "persons" in the divine substance Tertullian did not mean that God had three different personalities. Tertullian asserted that the three persons had but one purpose. He compared the Godhead to the

Roman government which at that time had three heads, Septimius Severus and his two associates. He wrote, "A unity that derives from itself a trinity is not destroyed but administered by it" (*Against Praxeas,* 3). According to Tertullian each of the individuals has full executive powers and exists simultaneously, yet the three accomplish one action. They are therefore one in unity.

Origen was more speculative than the jurist Tertullian, but he relied no less on Scripture to prove each point he made. Indeed, Origen left a greater number of Biblical commentaries than any other early father and is often, though perhaps improperly, called the first Christian exegete. In his attempt to explain the triune nature of God he insisted that there are three distinct entities in the Godhead, distinct but not separate. All three of these entities *(hypostaseis)* exist eternally. Justin and Tertullian merely suggested that the Son is generated from the Father, as light is from the sun, without getting involved in the problem of sequence, but Origen noted that if the Father is always the Father, there must always be a Son. Accordingly he spoke of the Son as "eternally generated." [10]

Neither the position of Tertullian nor that of Origen was popular in their day. They were accused of being too philosophical in their analysis of Scripture. Both were accused of tritheism by their opponents in the church. But it is ultimately their formulations that form the basis for the settlement of the problem in the fourth century — our Nicene Creed.

RESPONSIBILITY

The early teachers agreed with Irenaeus that salvation has its source in God and in the victory of Christ. But they stressed that ultimately each individual is responsible for either his salvation or damnation. Tertullian wrote that God does not choose to save an individual out of free grace, but rather because the individual has proved his worthiness:

[10] See his *Commentary on the Gospel of John,* II, i.

"What folly and perversity it is to practice an imperfect repentance and then to expect pardon for sin. This is like reaching out for the prize but not being willing to pay the price. The price that God has placed on the purchase of pardon is repentance. He offers impunity in exchange for repentance." [11] Tertullian also emphasized that after the grace of God has been accepted one must continue to cooperate with God to attain ultimate salvation. Man is judged and saved by his response to God's grace in Christ.

This stress on human responsibility for salvation or damnation can perhaps be explained by analyzing two of the situations that faced the early church.

There was a prevailing stress on morality in early Christian writings because the converts who came into the churches came with ethical standards far below those of God's Law. In Roman society humility was scorned and boasting with pride was the mark of the real man. Enlightened self-interest was the highest norm for the pagan rather than selfless concern for the needy brother. Revenge was the basic law of human relationships. Early Christian teachers could not assume that a man was married to only one woman, or that he was not keeping a number of mistresses. The Roman world took homosexuality lightly. For these reasons the apologists stressed how Christians were different from their pagan neighbors because they followed God's Law rather than any human regulations and whims. Tertullian wrote many tracts for the times and most of them deal with ethical and disciplinary matters.

A second and perhaps more important reason for early Christianity's stress on man's responsibility for his own salvation was the fact that the prevailing philosophies of the day tended to blame "cosmic structure" or "involuntary tendencies" and even "divine decrees" rather than man himself for his predicament. This thinking was also especially common among the Gnostics, who claimed that every event in human history was predetermined. The world was created

---

[11] *On Penance,* 6. See also Clement, *Stromateis,* III, 48; Origen, *On First Principles,* II, vii, 2; II, viii, 3.

and governed by invisible powers who controlled everything that took place on earth, including every human action. They pointed out that an individual is not born by choice, and that his race, social status, and mental qualities are all predetermined. This invisible plan that maps out the quality of man's desires beforehand also operates in the area of the spirit. Evil powers control the spiritual destiny of everyone except the "few" who are mysteriously chosen by a higher power to be saved, without any willed action on their part. The Gnostics taught that both salvation and damnation are beyond human control.

Because of the prevailing immorality and denial of human responsibility the early Christian teachers stressed the accountability of each man for his actions as well as for his salvation. Whenever the early fathers discussed man's salvation this was usually the context.

The emphasis on responsibility led to a number of accents in their thinking. First, if man is responsible for his life before God, he must have "free will" to exercise choice. They opposed the Gnostics who denied free will. In a lengthy discussion of the problem Clement of Alexandria wrote: "The Lord of all . . . uses persuasion on those who are willing; for it is not His way to compel one who is able of himself to obtain salvation by the exercise of free choice." [12] Second, the fathers avoided any suggestion that man's relationship to Adam so corrupted the human will that it had no power to choose the good. They allowed that as the result of Adam's sin all men have a tendency to evil and must necessarily die. But they said no more. They insisted that even though all men are born "in Adam" they have the ability to choose between right and wrong. There were a number of theories current about the precise nature of mankind's relationship to Adam's sin, but they all stressed that each individual is responsible for his own guilt. Justin Martyr wrote:

---

[12] *Stromateis,* VII, 6. See *Alexandrian Christianity,* ed. J. E. L. Oulton and H. Chadwick (Philadelphia: Westminster, 1954), p. 96.

So that none may infer from our belief in prophecy that everything takes place by inevitable destiny, I will explain. We learn from the prophets that both penalties and rewards are given according to the quality of each man's action. If this were not the case . . . nothing would be up to us. If it is destined that one should be good and another wicked, there is no reason to praise one and blame the other. If human beings do not have the free choice to choose what is right and avoid what is evil, then no one is responsible for his actions. (*1 Apology,* 43)

Third, early Christian teachers would not allow either philosopher or heretic to blame God as Creator for man's plight. The Gnostics claimed that man's dilemma was the result of certain weaknesses in creation itself. Christians, on the other hand, taught that creation is good and that only man is responsible for his condition. The corruption that prevails in life is not from creation but from man's perverted use of creation.

These concerns are the context of the statements of the fathers on salvation. Sometimes in their concern to preserve the integrity of both God and man they seem to ignore God's grace. This is not the case. Unlike Paul, however, who emphasized that man is declared just by God's grace for Christ's sake, the early Christians usually stressed "salvation" as the end product of God's grace and man's response.

RESURRECTION

The early Christians looked for the culmination of the reign of God in Christ's return to raise all men from the dead and in the establishment of the kingdom of the saints. The early writings, prayers, artwork, and tracts emphasized the sure character of this hope. Perhaps it was Paul himself who best summarized this firm conviction when he wrote, "But in fact Christ has been raised from the dead, the firstfruits of those who have fallen asleep" (1 Cor. 15:20 RSV). In the ancient world there were many myths about the gods' dying and rising from the dead to give immortal life to man, but none of these was based on historical fact. Peter also wrote, "We have been born anew to a living hope" (1 Peter

1:3 RSV). Personal life beyond death was one area where most pagans were never sure. They had many ideas about immortality, but they were rather vague. The Roman thinker Cicero, mourning the death of his daughter, wanted so much to be sure about her fate, but he had only a vague hope. Paul wrote that if Christians had no more than this, "we are of all men most to be pitied" (1 Cor. 15:19 RSV). Peter affirmed, "We have a sure hope," because it is based on the certainty of God's promise given in the resurrection of Jesus Christ from the dead. God does not lie!

In the face of strong Gnostic tendencies to deny the re-demptibility of the material creation, since it was not pro-duced by the true God, the emphasis of Christian teaching shifted in the second century from the joyous affirmation of a certain hope to a constant reiteration of the fact that it is the created body which will be resurrected.[13] Responding to philosophies that assumed merely the immortality of the soul and argued the impossibility of a decayed corpse being re-stored to life, the Christians stressed the resurrection of the body and produced many rational arguments to demonstrate the ability of God to perform this miracle (see *1 Clement*, 22—26). In this discussion, however, the Christians make it clear that they meant no more than that the identical body that had died would be resurrected. They were not concerned to affirm that the body would bear the same characteristics which it does now.[14] This insistence on identity is especially obvious when the apologists claimed that Christians, more than other people, were law-abiding since they knew that precisely the same body that commits the sin must answer for it before the divine judge.[15] When Origen pointed out that Christians teach the "resurrection of the body" rather than the "resurrection of the flesh," he was making the point that by bodily resurrection Christians do not teach that every aspect of the flesh will be the same, including the

---

[13] Tertullian, *On the Resurrection of the Flesh,* 3 f.

[14] Athenagoras, *On the Resurrection,* 3—9.

[15] Tertullian, *Apology,* 45; Athenagoras, *Plea,* 36.

injuries and defects, but rather emphasize that the *same* body, though in a glorified form, will be resurrected.[16] Origen encountered great difficulty and misunderstanding as a result of this distinction, but the debate illustrates the early Christian concern with identity and no more. It is precisely what God created that is redeemed and resurrected. Later this is summarized in the words, "I believe in the resurrection of the body."

It is unfortunate, perhaps, that the belief in resurrection should be the last item of the chapter. Actually it is among "the first things" that early Christians confessed. Everything the early Christians believed and did resulted in great part from their conviction that God won the decisive victory in Jesus Christ and through this action would bring men to glory.

---

[16] *On First Principles,* **II, 2, 2.**

V. CHURCH AND SOCIETY

NO ABIDING PLACE

The early Christian attitudes toward society cannot be understood apart from their views concerning the end of all things. Most primitive Christians believed that they were living in the last times and expected the *Parousia,* the triumphant return of Jesus, the culmination of all prophecy concerning the Kingdom, the visible reign of the Messiah, to take place in the immediate future. This did not happen. Jesus Himself had warned in His parables that they should not expect Him to return too quickly (see especially Matt. 24—25). Both Peter and Paul were forced to explain the delay to the early communities. (2 Peter 3; 1 Thess. 5)

After the period of the New Testament this attitude changed. Christians began to think of the "last things" as taking place primarily in the more distant future. They continued to repeat the old phrases about the end being near but didn't expect an immediate return of Christ. Indeed, in some cases they formulated intricate and imaginative time tables showing that there were still many years before Christ could return. These early Christian theorists, perhaps getting their ideas from Jewish apocalyptic speculations, believed that the world had to exist for 6,000 years. This calculation was based on the theory that each of the six days of creation equaled one thousand years. Claiming to have a special ability to interpret the Old Testament, a Christian writer who called himself Barnabas wrote, "Observe what 'He ended in six days' means. It means that in six thousand years the Lord will bring all things to an end, for a day with God is as a thousand years" (*Barnabas,* 15). Hippolytus, writing some time later, claimed that 5,500 of these years had already elapsed before the coming of Christ.[1] Since he lived in the first decades of the second century, he could not have expected Christ to return in his own lifetime.

While few early Christians went so far as to say that the world would last just 6,000 years, many of the early fathers did believe that when Christ returned He would reign here on earth for "a thousand years." Papias claimed to have heard this from a disciple of John.[2] Justin Martyr insisted:

> I and all other orthodox Christians know that there will be a resurrection of the flesh, and also a thousand years in Jerusalem built up and enlarged. . . . For it was said to Adam that in the day he should eat of the tree he should die. We know that he [Adam] did not live a thousand years. . . . And, further, a man among us named John, one of the apostles of Christ, prophesied in a revelation made to him that those who believed our Christ will spend a thousand years in Jerusalem, and afterwards the universal and eternal resurrection of all will take place. . . .[3]

To list all the early Christians who believed as did Justin and Papias would include most of the important names. There were those Christians, however, who did not accept this interpretation of the New Testament. Some went so far as to deny any historical occasion when *all* would be resurrected and judged at once. They reacted rather violently to these computing Christians. One of the most important in this number was the Alexandrian theologian Origen. He taught that judgment comes for each person when he is confronted by the Holy Spirit in his lifetime. If he refuses God's grace he is judged. On the other hand, if he accepts God's grace in Christ he is "born again to eternal life." All bodies will be resurrected individually to live eternally with God. It was not until the time of St. Augustine in the late fourth century that any synthesis of these views took place.

---

[1] *Commentary on Daniel,* IV, 23 ff.

[2] Eusebius, *Eccl. Hist.,* III, 39. See Rev. 20:4 for this reign. The term "millennialism," referring to the belief in this reign, comes from *millennium,* the Latin word for a period of a thousand years.

[3] *Dialogue with Trypho,* 80, 81.

Whether Christians were waiting for the immediate return of Christ, whether they merely looked forward to reigning with Him in the new Jerusalem someday, or simply hoped to be united with Him after death, they agreed that the present order of creation would be completely destroyed by fire. For this reason they had little interest in the improvement of society as such.

Modern Christians are often critical of the achievements of early Christianity in society because it didn't reconstruct society along Christian lines especially when it gained control in the fourth century. The Christians then had no intention of doing this. The achievements credited to Christianity in this area, and there are many, are merely a byproduct of their concern to live according to the will of God by loving others as they loved themselves. No other explanation is needed. Even to suggest that they couldn't change the institution of slavery assumes that they wanted to. They had no interest in what we today term "economic injustice," but they did care for the poor. Even military service gets amazingly little attention from the church fathers of this period. It has been suggested that they were opportunistic by not being critical of the existing social order. Perhaps. We would rather suggest that they had their eyes fixed on what Augustine called "the eternal city."

DISCIPLINE

The strict disciplinary procedures in the early Christian communities demonstrate their prevailing concern not to become engulfed by the corruption of the pagan society surrounding them. The church protected each individual within the group from "being turned aside" through a strong emphasis on "holy living" and through confession of gross deviations before the congregation or its leaders.[4] Once admitted into the church through Baptism the Christian was expected to avoid all sin. If he became guilty of grave sin he was expected to confess it and prove his sorrow by becoming a public peni-

[4] Heb. 2:1-4; 10:24, 25; 12:1-4; James 5:16.

tent. The status of such a penitent was somewhat analogous to that of a catechumen. Temporarily placed outside the community of the faithful, he was refused the Holy Eucharist. During this period of exclusion he was to indicate his repentance by abstaining from all pleasure such as ornate dress and sexual intercourse. Tertullian describes the penitential acts as follows:

> [The penitent] must lie in sackcloth and ashes, cover himself with rags and sorrow. This severe treatment is an exchange for the sins committed. He must take only the necessary food and drink. . . . Praying, fasting, groaning, crying out to God, prostrating himself before the elders and kneeling before other members of the congregation, as he pleads with them to carry his name before God. True Confession does all this to make repentance acceptable and to honor God by showing fear. This serves as a substitute for God's wrath and, as it were, exchanges temporal mortification for eternal punishment.[5]

The penance assigned to a person was gauged according to the character of the sin. The actual decision was made by the individual bishop. It is not until the Middle Ages that this process is standardized through the Irish Penitentials. Only after a protracted period of such penance was the penitent allowed to participate in the Eucharist through a public "reconciliation," which consisted of a prayer and the "laying on of hands" by the bishop.

One of the most difficult problems the church faced in the third century was determining which grave sin could be granted the privilege of such "repentance" and the number of times this should be allowed. This became especially acute when dealing with the members who had "lapsed" or fallen off during persecution.

In the early persecutions individuals who confessed to being Christians were simply executed. They were called "martyrs," that is, "witnesses." In the third century, however, there were so many Christians that to kill them would have decimated the population. Since the Roman government could not afford to practice this sort of thing, the Christians

---

[5] *On Repentance,* 9.

were tortured until they denied Christ by saying "Caesar is Lord" instead of "Christ is Lord." If a Christian sustained this persecution without denying Christ he was called a "confessor." Such an individual was ranked with the presbyters, evidently endowed with a special gift of the Spirit for the witness he had borne.[6] If a believer under torture did what the Romans demanded, he was classed among the "lapsed." Could the church accept the subsequent repentance of those who had lapsed? At first it seemed beyond the church's powers to restore lapsed members to a participation in the holy things of God which they seemed to have spurned (see Heb. 3:7-19). They had, some asserted, committed the "sin against the Holy Spirit" (see Matt. 12:31, 32). Since the Romans often tortured an individual to deny more than once, the question also arose how many times denial could be forgiven if it was to be forgiven at all.

A number of positions were taken on this question. The strict position was exemplified by the schismatic Montanists and Novatians (200—235), who classified falling away as the sin against the Spirit and refused the Eucharist to those repenting, even on their deathbed. The Novatians separated themselves from the rest of the church when it decided to receive the lapsed who repented of their action. The Gnostic Christians, on the other extreme, distinguished denial by the mouth from denial in the heart and took such lapsing rather lightly. The church as a whole finally took the middle position of granting the lapsed the possibility of "repentance," sometimes once, sometimes twice, but always under severe restrictions. They feared that greater lenience would encourage Christians not to take such lapses seriously and tempt them to try to take advantage of God's grace.[7] The seriousness with which the Christian communities dealt with the lapsed illustrates the attitude of the early church toward gross sins.

---

[6] See Mark 13:11. See also Hippolytus, I, 10.

[7] *The Shepherd of Hermas,* Mandate 4, 3; Clement, *Stromateis,* II, xiii, 56; Tertullian, *On Repentance,* 7.

BE YE SEPARATE

That the Christians were aloof from pagan society is illustrated by their attitude toward Roman entertainment. The arena, circus, and theater seem to have been avoided completely. The theaters were infamous to the Christian mind because they portrayed immorality among gods and men. Gossip had it that only women of light virtue played in these productions. The Romans also had a custom of substituting criminals where the script demanded that a killing take place. Indeed, Nero forced Christians to play various mythological roles both to amuse the crowds and also as a form of public execution.

Perhaps the worst form of amusement among the Romans was the gladiatorial combat. This was big business. At one point in the second century over half the days in the year were taken up with such shows in the arena. They were free to the populace and became so common that mere races and other forms of athletics were too tame for the people. Roman officials vied with each other to put on the biggest and the best show for the people. It was a way to keep the government popular with the masses. Entrepreneurs trained men to fight in these shows. Often they were captives who had no choice. Not until the third century were laws passed forbidding anyone to force a slave into the arena. In these gladiatorial combats the crowd took sides. Often the winner of one bout would be pitted against other winners until only one or two were left from a field of men. As many as 200 pairs a day would fight. If a free man won such a round, he could earn enough to spend the rest of his life in ease. This type of combat was also used by the Roman government to execute criminals.

The Christian attitude toward such amusements is illustrated by Tertullian's tract *On Shows*. He warned the newly baptized of the danger involved: "It is not by being merely in the world that we fall from faith, but by touching and tainting ourselves with the world's sins. To go to the circus or the theater as a spectator is no different from sacrificing in the temple of Serapis." (*On Shows,* 8.) Admitting there was no divine command forbidding attendance, Tertullian quoted the First Psalm, "Blessed is the man who walks not in the counsel of the wicked." His main reason for forbidding this activity, however, was the idolatry associated with it. He pointed out that the gladiatorial combats and the races were dedicated to the gods. Recalling that Christians did not eat food offered to idols, he continued: "If we keep our throats and bellies free from defilement, how much more should we withhold our nobler parts, our ears and eyes, from such enjoyments. This idolatry does not merely pass through the body, but is digested by our very souls and spirits. God has a right to claim purity here even more than in our body" (ibid., 13). "From the sky to the sty" was the way he curtly cut off all further debate, and pleaded for complete separation: "Would that we did not even inhabit the same world with such people! While that wish cannot be realized, we are separated from the worldly. The world is God's, but the worldly is the devil's." (Ibid., 25 and 15)

Tertullian's statements were often in the extreme. But the attitude he represented was rather common. Athenagoras put it just as clearly, "We see little difference between watching a man being put to death and killing him. We have given up such spectacles" (*Plea,* 35). Tatian was perhaps the most bitter about the theater, "They carouse in affected manner, going through many indecent movements; your sons and daughters behold them giving lessons in adultery on the stage." (*Oration,* 23)

This separateness is also illustrated in the early Christian attitude toward military and civil service. Such service was of course the pride of the Roman citizen. The classical mind considered the well-organized state as the highest condition of well-being. This did not mean that the individual was unimportant — they were most concerned with the individual's cultural development — but the concerns of the individual were subordinated to those of society. The important "virtues" and "duties" were political in character.

It seems that some Christians may have served in the military prior to the end of the second century, but they were apparently individuals who had been in either civil or military service prior to their conversion.[8] Tertullian (c. 200) argued from the fact that there were Christians in government work: "We are a new group but have already penetrated all areas of imperial life — cities, islands, villages, towns, market-places, even the camp, tribes, palace, senate, the law-court. There is nothing left for you but your temples" (*Apology,* 37). To show that Christians were really good citizens he pleaded: "We live in the world with you. We do not forsake forum . . . or bath . . . or workshop, or inn, or market, or any other place of commerce. We sail with you, fight with you, farm with you. . . ." (*Apology,* 42)

By the end of the second century, however, the fathers, including Tertullian, opposed such service. It is quite possible that Christians were not drafted before this time since they were generally from the noncitizen classes before Caracalla (212) lowered the property requirements for citizenship. From *The Apostolic Tradition* (200) we gather that Hippolytus reluctantly allowed an individual to remain a soldier if he was converted in the army, but he did not allow an individual to join the army after his baptism. Tertullian contended that Christians were not useful to the army because they would rather be killed than kill. "A Christian cannot serve two masters," he wrote:

> People ask whether a baptized Christian can become a soldier or whether a soldier may be admitted to the faith. . . . One might suggest in jest that Moses carried a rod and Aaron wore a buckle, John had a leather belt, Joshua led an army, and Peter made war. But you tell me how Peter could have served in war, indeed even in peacetime, without a sword? Even if soldiers did come to John, and the centurion did believe, the Lord Himself unbelted every soldier when He took the sword from Peter. (*On Idolatry,* 19)

His attitude was the same when he discussed civil service:

> Can a servant of God fill an administrative office if by favor or ingenuity he avoids any form of idolatry, as Joseph

8 Acts 8:27; 10:1; 13:12; 16:27-34; 18:8; Phil. 4:22; Rom. 16:10, 11.

and Daniel governed Egypt and Babylon without being corrupted by idolatry? If a man can hold his office and never
sacrifice, never authorize sacrifice, never contract for sacrificial victims, never administer the supervision of the temple,
never handle temple taxes, never plan a show either his own
or the state's, never preside over one, never announce or
order a [pagan] festival, never take an oath, never be responsible for capital punishment or loss of civil status (one
might inflict a fine), never execute, or torture, or im-
prison; if he can avoid all these things he may hold office!
(Ibid., 17)

Origen in another part of Africa took the same position.
To Celsus' charge that Christians avoided these responsibil-
ities out of fear or lack of patriotism, Origen asserted that
Christians perform greater service to the state when they
serve as officials in the church and especially when they pray
for the government.[9] When Origen was asked what would
happen if the majority of people in the world were Christian,
he deduced that there would obviously be no more war.
In any case, Origen agreed with Tertullian that nothing is
more alien to the Christian than politics and military service.
It is difficult to say how strong the opposite opinion on this
subject was during this period. It was certainly not as ably
presented, if presented at all.

LOVE THY NEIGHBOR

Christian writers from this period exhibit little concern about
the institution of slavery. When they do speak of it, it is in
terms of loving all men as brothers. This expressed itself
mainly in the treatment of slaves but also in either setting
them free or buying their freedom.

Slavery was an accepted part of the Roman political and
economic system. Slaves were usually captured enemy sol-
diers, and in the centuries before Christ an owner had abso-
lute control over them. They could be sold, lent, given, be-
queathed, or killed. In the second century after Christ legislation made the institution more humane. Allowed to share

[9] *Against Celsus,* VIII, 73—75.

in the growing wealth of the empire, many slaves accumulated enough wealth to purchase their freedom. Laws were passed forbidding the use of slaves in the public games, easing manumission of slaves no longer needed or sick, making the murder of a slave a crime like any other murder, and giving the slave a right to bring grievances before a court of law.

The Stoic philosophers were in the forefront of this movement for humane treatment. Cicero differed from the ancient Greek philosopher Aristotle by insisting that all men are equal, since they have the ability to differentiate right from wrong. Seneca, a Roman contemporary of Christ, taught that slaves had the same nature as their master because they could develop in virtue. The slave should realize, Seneca thought, that bondage was merely external, and the master should treat a slave more like a servant.

Actually the Christian fathers said little more than this, but they put it into practice by urging the Christian master to treat a slave as his brother. Aristides wrote: "Slaves, male and female, are encouraged to be instructed in Christianity on account of the love their masters have for them. When this happens, they are called brethren without any distinction" (*Apology,* 15). When Euelpistes, a slave in the imperial household, was brought before the tribunal of Rusticus with Justin Martyr, he explained his status, "I am a slave of the emperor, but I am also a Christian and have received liberty from Jesus Christ; by His grace I have the same hope as my brethren." [10] No slave was allowed to accept baptism without an attestation of character from his owner if the latter was a Christian; but once the slave was baptized, he could become even a clergyman. At least one ex-slave, Callistus, became bishop of Rome. (C. 220)

That Christians owned slaves is obvious from the records we have, but they encouraged manumission. Congregations set aside funds to purchase the freedom of slaves (Ignatius, *To Polycarp,* 4). There was a special ceremony for manumission in Christian communities. The master led the slave

---

[10] *The Martyrdom of Justin and His Companions,* 4.

to the altar, where the document of emancipation was read. After the bishop pronounced the blessing he was received as a free brother by the congregation. The early Christians were warned to stay away from public meetings unless they attended to purchase the freedom of a slave. One individual freed some 1,250 slaves on the day of his baptism, and this is not the only recorded incident of this kind.

The works of charity that Christians accomplished in the Roman Empire continue to be one of the greatest stars in the church's crown. Even the pagans noticed this. Lucian, who is known more for his satire than his appreciation, wrote: "It is incredible to see the ardor with which the people of that religion help each other in their wants. They spare nothing. Their first legislator (Jesus) has put into their heads that they are all brethren." [11]

The classical world had little concern for the sick and poor. Plato suggested that allowing the poor to die shortened their misery. Cicero allowed help only to those who would receive such charity to improve themselves. There is a hint of this same attitude in some Christian literature. The Didachist exhorted the Christian to allow the gift to "burn in the hand" until he knows to whom he is giving it (*Didache,* 1:6). The position of Hermas, however, seems to be the more normal. He wrote that it is in the attitude of the giver that God finds pleasure, not in how the gift is used.[12]

From the beginning Christians shared their wealth. There is no suggestion, except in Acts, that wealth be redistributed or that poverty is an injustice, but a common fund was set up in each congregation to which all contributed as they could for the benefit of the poor. The original practice in the Jerusalem community continued to exercise an influence: "Now the company of those who believed were of one heart

---

[11] *The Passing of Peregrinus,* 13.

[12] Mandate 2:4-6. See Vision III, vi, 5—7; ix, 2—6. See also Clement of Alexandria, *Whether a Rich Man Can Be Saved,* 37, 38; Athenagoras, *Plea,* 35.

and soul, and no one said that any of the things which he possessed was his own, but they had everything in common. . . . There was not a needy person among them, for as many as were possessors of lands or houses sold them and brought the proceeds . . . and distribution was made to each as they had need" (Acts 4:32-35 RSV). This, however, was unique in early Christianity; the rest of the church did not follow this example. The example they followed was one of *continuing* to share their wealth with those less fortunate. Justin Martyr informs the emperor that "we who once took pleasure in the means of increasing our wealth and property now bring what we have into a common fund and share with everyone in need." (*1 Apology,* 14)

Christians practiced this charity both among themselves and toward others. Aristides informed the emperor, "He who has gives to him who has not without grudging, and when they see a stranger they bring him to their dwellings and rejoice over him as a true brother" (*Apology,* 15). Hospitality to strangers was important in a day when inns were not desirable places. Ancient society did not provide care for orphans but allowed them to be raised for prostitution or other disreputable occupations. Christians made these unfortunates the object of their concern. Since the only hospitals in existence were private or associated with religious cults, Christians also took care of the sick. During plagues in Carthage and Alexandria around the middle of the third century the Christians cared for the suffering even after the pagans had abandoned them. A contemporary description of Christian charity in time of plague written by the bishop in Alexandria reports:

> Most of our brethren . . . visited the sick without thought as to the danger. . . . Most gladly departed this life along with them, being infected with the disease from others. . . . They would take up the bodies of the dead and place their hands properly, closing their eyes and shutting their mouths . . . bathing them, and finally lay them out in burial clothes. After a while they received the same services themselves. The conduct of the heathen was altogether different. They deserted those who began to be sick and

fled from their dearest ones. They would leave them half
dead and treat corpses as vile refuse. Anything to avoid
contact.[13]

MARRIAGE AND SEX

The Christian attitude toward sexual morality and their interpretation of the nature of marriage was radical. Pagan
philosophers and religious teachers talked about moral purity,
but did not regard sexual immorality with the same degree
of seriousness as did the Christian teachers; the family sta-
bility and moral discipline of ancient Rome were giving way
to decadence.

It is perhaps important to pause here for a moment to
emphasize the ascetic character of early Christianity and to
point out that this asceticism did not deny the original goodness or redemptibility of the physical. In the face of Gnostic
assertions that the body is evil since it is part of the physical
creation, the Christians taught that it was not the body itself
that was evil, but rather the irrational and selfish will within
man which failed to curb his lusts and passions. Early Christian asceticism then is not a Gnostic negation of creation but
rather an attempt to give God's creation back to Him in
a good and holy state, not perverted by the will of man.
The church's attitude toward sex is an illustration of it.

Monogamy was the rule among the Romans. Adultery, or
sexual union with the wife of another Roman citizen, was
severely punished. Yet, although allowed only one wife, a
married Roman was free to have sexual intercourse with a
mistress, a prostitute, or even with his male and female slaves.
The wife did not have these privileges. While divorce was
not common among the Romans at the time of early Christianity, Seneca still could write, "No woman need blush about
breaking her marriage since the most prominent ladies have
learned to reckon the year by the names of their husbands." [14]

Christians were much more severe in their demands for

---

[13] Eusebius, *Eccl. Hist.*, VII, 22, 1 ff.

[14] *On Benefits*, III, xvi, 2.

marital faithfulness. Any coition outside of marriage was considered grave sin. Many felt that after baptism adultery could be forgiven only once if at all. Early Christian teachers suggested that the purpose of sexual intercourse was merely to produce children. They contrasted their attitude with that of the pagan, who undertook it "to satisfy his lust." Monogamy in the early church meant that a man was to have only one wife at a time, but many also believed that he was to make only one such contract in his lifetime.

Christian teachers regularly quoted the words which Jesus addressed to His disciples and in which He forbade divorce except because of fornication (Matt. 19:9). But they insisted that the permission to divorce here meant merely separation since there is no permission to remarry. They also quoted St. Paul to effect that widows do better to remain unmarried (1 Cor. 7:8, 9). These attitudes occur in the earliest literature outside of the New Testament. Polycarp (115) wrote about widows who were "pledged to the Lord," and Ignatius greeted "the virgins enrolled with the widows." [15] Hermas in Rome (c. 100) stressed that believers ought not automatically seek divorce for adultery since spouses might be able to help each other overcome evil. Hermas did not treat adultery lightly, for he was not sure that it is even forgivable after baptism; but he encouraged the injured party to show Christian love even here and discouraged second marriage in any case (Mandate, 4:4). Rejoicing that "those who once rejoiced in fornication now delight in continence alone," and that "many men and women now in their sixties and seventies, disciples of Christ from their youth, have preserved their purity," Justin Martyr suggested, "Those who make second marriages according to human law are sinners in the sight of our Teacher." [16]

Some early Christians, especially those with tendencies toward Gnosticism or Montanism, were even more severe. Tatian condemned the marriage relationship itself as de-

[15] *Smyrnaeans*, 13:1; *To Polycarp*, 4:3.
[16] *1 Apology*, 15. See also Athenagoras, *Plea*, 33.

structive of prayer life.[17]   In a letter to his wife Tertullian
caustically questioned whether their marriage was really for
the best.   He calls their sexual relation a "voluptuous dis-
grace" and suggested that it certainly ought not to be repeated.   The death of a spouse is God's call to continence
for the other (*To Wife,* 2:2; 1:7).   He noted that in the old
dispensation under Adam men were encouraged to marry,
but in the new covenant we follow the example of Christ who
did not marry (*On Monogamy,* 7—11).   Such extremists in
an earlier period seem to have prompted the censure of Paul,
"In later times some will depart from the faith by giving
heed to deceitful spirits . . . who forbid marriage. . . ."
(1 Tim. 4:3)

Clement of Alexandria's appreciation of both celibacy
and marriage as gifts from God, as well as his willingness to
allow second marriage if necessary, is more representative
of early Christianity: "We welcome the blessed state of ab-
stinence from marriage among those who have been granted
the gift by God.   We admire monogamy and the single marriage because we need to share suffering and also bear one
another's burdens. . . . Of second marriage the apostle writes,
'You may, if you burn.' " [18]

The early Christians universally taught that the first purpose of marriage was to have children.   The Romans had the
custom of exposing children they did not desire.   A letter
from the period of our Lord written by a pagan in Egypt
shows the cold, matter-of-fact character of this custom when
it directs: "When you give birth to your child, if it is a boy,
let it live; if it is a girl, expose it."   The philosopher Seneca
explained, "We destroy monstrous offspring; if they are born
feeble or ill-formed, we drown them.   It is not wrath but
reason that separates the useless from the healthy."   In the
face of this attitude Christians insisted that they did not
marry except to bring up children; and if they didn't desire
children, they abstained from sex.[19]

---

[17] Lost work quoted in Clement, *Stromateis,* III, 81.
[18] *Stromateis,* III, i, 4.
[19] Justin Martyr, *1 Apology,* 29; Athenagoras, *Plea,* 35.

The church fathers revealed another purpose of marriage, that of mutual spiritual support, when they condemned mixed marriages. Tertullian wrote about this to his wife: "How can I paint the happiness in a marriage that the church ratifies, the celebration of Communion confirms, the benediction seals. . . ? What a union! . . . They pray together, fast together, instruct, exhort, and support each other. . . . They share each other's tribulation, persecution, and revival. . . . They delight to visit the sick, help the needy, give alms freely. . . . Christ rejoices when He hears and sees this" (*To Wife,* 2:8). It is this ideal of marriage that led Tertullian to question whether a mixed marriage ought even be contemplated. He asked whether a heathen would allow his wife to attend night meetings, participate in the slandered Supper of the Lord, take care of the sick in the poorest hovels, kiss the chains of martyrs in prison, rise in the night for prayer, or show hospitality to strange brethren.

Early Christianity did not attempt to change any social or economic structures. Therefore the church cannot be scorned for having effected so few changes in them. No voice was raised against the institution of slavery. Wars continued to be fought; Christians even participated. What was revolutionary about the social outlook of the early Christians was their adherence to God's will that they love their fellowmen rather than selfishly entangle themselves in the things of this world. There was a necessary tension here. They avoided any pagan activities that would tend to betray their moral code. But at the same time the early Christians worked hard, gave much, and treated all men of whatever station as "brothers."

The Christians looked for the end of the age and as a result were not interested in social structures, but they were at the same time deeply committed to the welfare of their fellowmen. An eschatological involvement!

VI. CHURCH AND STATE

THE SETTING

Christianity entered a world in which it was taken for granted that the state dominated religious activities. Prior to the advent of Christianity the Romans made no distinction between the life of the state and the religious life of the people. The Romans felt that the gods had given them empire, peace, and prosperity as a result of their being pleased with the worship they received from the Romans. Cicero admitted that it was because the Romans surpassed all others in piety that the gods had protected and prospered the empire. Horace insisted that the Romans owed their empire to their submission to the gods and attributed the ills of Rome to the neglect of the temples. The maintenance of this covenant was the responsibility of the state. The priests appointed by the Senate carried out the ritual worship under the direction of the *pontifex maximus*. The people had little to do with this worship except on festivals. The citizen, however, was expected to do nothing that would displease the gods of Rome. In his home and on his farm every Roman had altars dedicated to the traditional gods of Rome. This family worship took the form of various rites that had to be carefully carried out.

Since the oversight was in the hands of the Senate, only gods whose cult was allowed by the Senate could legally be worshiped. Whenever the Roman armies incorporated a new area into the Roman state, the Senate would add the statues of the gods of that territory to the Pantheon. As the empire expanded, people from all over the Mediterranean moved to Rome, bringing the worship of their own gods with them. Since these gods had not received the official sanction of the Senate they were designated as "private" gods. Worshiped by the people rather than by officially appointed priests, they were not related to the most ancient religious traditions of the Roman people. The cults were often of the "mystery" type.

The *mystery religions* emphasized the assurance of personal immortality through personal relationship with deity. This experience took place when the initiate into the cult was allowed to view the mystery of death and the restoration to life presented in dramatic form. The ritual drama was the "mystery." The most popular of the deities involved in the mystery cults were Isis and Osiris from Egypt, Attis and Cybele from Asia Minor, and Demeter from Greece. The dramas differed in particulars, but essentially each recounted the "mystery" of how the deity suffered death, was forced to reside in Hades for a time, but ultimately triumphed over death through a resurrection. The myths reenacted here originally concerned the annual death and rebirth in nature. The gods were involved in the recurring advent of winter and the birth of spring. Only later were the myths viewed as the key to an eternal life for human beings. After an individual had witnessed this drama he was a "knowing one." The ritual connected with this initiation included washings, eating the flesh of slain animals, and in some mysteries participating in various orgiastic activities such as wild dancing, being drenched in blood, mutilating oneself, and sexual license.

The Roman government carefully watched these cults to prevent any citizen from participating in immorality. The immoral rites of Cybele were permitted in Rome, but no Roman was allowed to participate. The police were often called to break up gatherings for the worship of Dionysus, the god of wine, because of the immoral practices involved. The Roman government was also concerned about the possibility that these foreign cults might be a breeding ground for sedition since they were very popular with the disinherited in Rome.

It was not tolerance that caused Rome to allow these forms of worship but rather the popular demand for them. Indeed, just before Christianity began to be popular in Rome, the government attempted to reestablish its control of popular religious life by introducing a new cult to preserve the religious traditions of Rome through the worship of "the spirit of Rome" in the person of the emperor. "Deity" was usually not defined philosophically, but was seen as that which gives good things. Since Rome brought peace and justice, it was honored and praised or worshiped. But what was the symbol of imperial Rome? The person of the emperor was the obvious choice. Hence the emperor cult. The Romans gave to the emperor honor and praise as the incarnation of all that made Rome great and all that Rome did for the world. The names of most of the traditional gods of Rome were attached in one way or another to this cult. Generally speaking, however, the emperors did not think of themselves as gods walking on the earth. Rather they participated in deity to the degree that their wills determined the course of peoples' lives through their office. This cult became rather popular, even though the people were not expected to participate in these rites before the third century.

Since Christianity was not the official religion of any state with which the Romans came into contact and was therefore a private and unofficial cult, it developed as an institution entirely separate from the state.

CONFLICT AND MARTYRDOM

The attitude of Roman society toward Christians was one of suspicion. Since Christianity began in Palestine and many of the early Christians were Jews, the Roman populace simply transferred to the church their detestation of the Jew. The Christians could show no image of their God and denied the existence of the gods. The Romans deduced from this that they were "atheists." When Christians spoke of eating the "body" and drinking the "blood" of the "Son," the Romans gossiped that they were butchering babies and eating their flesh and blood. Fronto, the teacher of Marcus Aurelius, wrote:

> Now the story of their initiating novices is as detestable as it is notorious. An infant, concealed in meal so as to deceive the unwary, is placed before the one who is in charge of the rites. This infant, hidden under the meal, is struck by the novice, who thinks he is striking harmless blows but kills him with blind and hidden wounds. Horrible to relate, they drink his blood, eagerly distributing the members of his body, and are united by this sacrifice and pledged to common silence by their awareness of guilt. . . . Everyone knows about their banquet, and everyone speaks of it. People of both sexes and every age come to the banquet on the accustomed day with the children, sisters, mothers. There, after much feasting when the banquet has grown warm and the heat of drunkenness burns into incestuous desire, a dog tied to the lampstand is aroused to run and jump by throwing a bit of food beyond the length of the rope by which he is tied. Thus with the light . . . overturned and put out, the haphazard embraces of shameful desire take place in the shameless darkness.[1]

This was the rumor among the Romans. The good qualities of the Christians were lost in this mire of suspicion and gossip. Suetonius suggested that the Christians were "superstitious," a word associated with witchcraft. Tacitus called them "haters of the human race" because they didn't worship any known or knowable god and practiced immoral rites.

It was only natural that Nero should play on the suspicions of the people and blame the fire in Rome (64) on Christians. We do not know who started that blaze. Nero, however, made the mistake of rebuilding the burned part of the city and constructing many beautiful temples. The people suspected that he was building temples to placate the wrath of the gods for his having destroyed part of their city. To turn suspicion from himself he picked a small foreign group in Rome that everyone suspected of the most horrible crimes

[1] Quoted from Robert Grant, *The Sword and the Cross* (New York: Macmillan, 1955), pp. 75, 76.

and hated for their aloofness from most social activities, blamed them for the fire, and encouraged against them the wrath of the populace. Even Tacitus thought the punishment severe: "Besides being put to death they were made to serve as objects of amusement; they were clad in the hides of beasts and torn to death by dogs; some were crucified, others set on fire to serve to illuminate the night when daylight failed" (*Annals*, XV, 44). Most Romans regarded such execution of criminals as routine. Peter and Paul probably lost their lives in this persecution.

Following the pattern of Nero's day, persecution spread to other areas of the empire at the turn of the century. John was exiled to the island of Patmos. The grandchildren of Jude were called to Rome by Domitian to determine whether his suspicions were true. Ignatius, bishop of Antioch, and Polycarp, bishop of Smyrna, were martyred in the midst of celebrating and cheering mobs. In Lyons about 50 Christians were mobbed. The Christians who suffered described it to their brethren in Asia:

> But these rumors spread, and all were infuriated at us. . . . But the entire fury of the crowd, governor, and soldiers fell on Sanctus, the deacon from Vienne, and on Maturus, a noble combatant though but lately baptized, and on Attalus, a native of Pergamum . . . and on Blandina. . . . Blandina was filled with such power that those who by turns kept torturing her in every way from dawn till evening were worn out and exhausted, and themselves confessed defeat from lack of ought else to do to her; they marvelled that the breath still remained in her body all mangled and covered with gaping wounds. . . . But the blessed woman . . . in confession regained her youth; and for her to say, "I am a Christian, and with us no evil finds a place" was refreshment.[2]

There were no empire-wide centrally directed persecutions until the third century. Before this time persecution was sporadic and local. The government usually acted when encouraged by the mob. Officials did not seek out Christians. Only if an individual was accused of being "Christian" was

2 Eusebius, *Eccl. Hist.*, V, 1.

he liable to police action. It was assumed that if he confessed to "the name," he was guilty of all the actions that
gossip credited to Christianity. For this reason Peter wrote,
"If one suffers as a *Christian,* let him not be ashamed, but
under that name let him glorify God." (1 Peter 4:16 RSV)

The courage of Christians who faced diabolical tortures
earned the admiration of both Roman and fellow Christian.
Tertullian wrote, "the blood of Christians is seed" (*Apology,*
50), indicating that many were converted who witnessed
the death of these "athletes of God." [3] The term "martyr"
meant "witness" in Greek. Originally, any Christian who
suffered for the faith, whether he was or was not executed,
was spoken of as such a "martyr" or "confessor." The
memory of these martyrs who went all the way with Christ
was honored in the churches. They were the highest expression of Christian selflessness. And more, they symbolized
the belief that a true confessor or prophet must suffer, as
Jesus said: "He who does not take his cross and follow Me
is not worthy of Me. He who finds his life will lose it,
and he who loses his life for My sake will find it" (Matt.
10:38, 39 RSV). Irenaeus thought of Jesus as the Master
Martyr.[4] Origen wrote: "As we behold the martyrs coming
forth from every church to be brought before the tribunal,
we see in each the Lord Himself condemned." When Ignatius
heard that the Christians in Rome hoped to prevent his
execution, he wrote:

> It is as a prisoner for Jesus Christ that I hope to greet
> you. . . . May I have the good fortune to meet my fate
> without interference! What I fear is your generosity, which
> may prove detrimental to me. For you can easily do what
> you want to, whereas it is hard for me to get to God unless
> you let me alone. . . . Grant me no more than to be a sacri-
> fice for God while there is an altar at hand. . . . I am
> corresponding with all the churches and bidding them all
> to realize that I am voluntarily dying for God — that is,
> if you do not interfere. I plead with you, do not do me
> an unseasonable kindness. Let me be fodder for the wild

---

[3] See 1 Cor. 9:24-27; *Martyrdom of Polycarp,* 18:3.

[4] *Against Heresies,* III, xviii, 5.

beasts — that is how I can get to God. I am God's wheat and I am being ground by the teeth of wild beasts to make a pure loaf for Christ.[5]

Shrines developed around the relics of martyrs. The places where they lived or were buried, articles they used, and their bones were held in high honor and became centers of devotion.[6] The anniversaries of the local martyrs' deaths were celebrated by the Christian communities as these heroes' heavenly "birthdays." Since early Christians believed that martyrs had a special status "with the Lord" (see Rev. 6: 9-11), their lives and prayers served as intercession for those still on earth. While seeking martyrdom was generally discouraged, the high regard in which it was held is indicated by the fact that it was called a second baptism.

CHRISTIAN ATTITUDES TOWARD THE STATE

To explain their position, some Christians in the second century wrote Apologies (*apologia* meaning "defense") to the emperor in which they declared that they were not atheists, immoral, or unpatriotic. Justin admitted that Christians did not worship the gods, but he insisted that this did not mean that they were atheists. He explains that there is only one God, and this is the God Christians worship. Since the Christians were suspected of disloyalty to the state because they spoke of Jesus as "Lord," a title assumed by the emperor, Justin also attempted to show that when Christians talked about a kingdom of Christ, they were not necessarily disloyal to the empire (*1 Apology*, 11). It is important to note, however, that the millennialistic (see p. 72) teaching of early Christianity certainly gave cause, unjust though it was, to these suspicions. Tertullian pointed out that Christians refused to worship the emperor because he was not God, but he insisted that Christians were loyal to the emperor.

---

[5] *To the Romans*, 1—2. See Richardson, p. 103.

[6] See *Martyrdom of Polycarp*, 16—19; Eusebius, *Eccl. Hist.*, V, i, 57—63. See also p. 90.

Aristides also defended Christians against the charge of immorality: "Wherefore they do not commit adultery nor fornication, nor bear false witness, nor embezzle what is held in pledge, nor covet what is not theirs. . . . And their women, O Emperor, are pure as virgins, and their daughters are modest; and their men keep themselves from every unlawful union and from all uncleanness" (*Apology,* 15). Theophilus claimed that on the basis of such evidence the Christians were actually the empire's best citizens (*To Autolycus,* 9 to 15). Both Justin and Tertullian included descriptions of Christian worship to prove that it was not immoral.

These apologists pleaded for toleration of Christians. They justified this in a number of ways. Athenagoras suggested that Christians were like any other philosophical group and should be accepted as such (*Plea,* 2). Justin Martyr appealed to the generally accepted idea that Rome stood for justice, insisting that to allow mobs to control legal procedures was not justice. Certainly the emperor could not allow Christians to be executed without a fair trial in which all the evidence was laid out. Justin seems rather sure that a fair trial would exonerate the Christians (*1 Apology,* 4, 7). But these earlier apologists requested toleration only for themselves. They did not argue from a basic principle of "rights." Tertullian was the first to demand freedom to worship for all individuals on the basis of a fundamental human right. He contended that it was a privilege of nature to worship God as one pleased. He did not urge that the state withdraw from the religious life of the community but merely suggested that it ought not to attempt to control *how* an individual worshiped God (*To Scapula,* 2). This was not an uncommon idea among pagans in the fourth century; it is rather interesting coming from a Christian.

The early fathers accepted the divine function of government. The function of the state, according to Irenaeus, is to reward good and punish evil. This is necessary because of sin. "Since man, departing from God, reached such a pitch of fury that he looked upon his own brother as an enemy and engaged in all kinds of restless conduct without fear, God

imposed upon man the fear of man." [7] God uses the state
to curb the passions of men and to bring some degree of
justice to human life. Generally the fathers quoted Paul's
emphasis on government as "God's servant." [8] Set in the
midst of a section on Christian love, Paul's remarks in Romans 13 illustrated the relationship between those who live
according to love and the institution that exists by force.
Paul asserts that government carries out a divine function,
even if it does not do it in love.

While the fathers thought of government as having a divine function, they also thought of it basically as a "human
institution," resulting from sin. By the fourth century many
Christians considered man's original condition as one "without government." There are some indications of this view
in the second century. Tatian suggested that this world was
created "good," but the organized human conduct that makes
up society is bad. He classed civilization and government
together as perversions of the original cosmos (*Oration,* 19).
Tertullian, challenging the idea that Rome's greatness was the
result of divine favor, asserted that the Roman Empire was
the product of war and bloodshed (*Apology,* 25). Hippolytus had little or nothing good to say about the Roman Empire, for he compared it to wild beasts that ravage among
peaceful people.[9] That Rome should rule the world seemed
but a satanic aping of the catholic kingdom of Christ. Government he considered at most an evil, but a necessary one.
This attitude was augmented when the fathers connected government with the coming of Antichrist (Rev. 13). Hippolytus also pointed out that the Antichrist would arise out
of the tribe of Dan, overwhelm the 10 kingdoms into which
the Roman Empire would be subdivided, and finally, in alli-
ance with these various parts of the empire, war against
Christ.[10] Both Hippolytus and Tertullian assumed that the

[7] Irenaeus, *Against Heresies,* V, 24.

[8] See Origen, *Comm. on Rom.,* IX, 26—28; Athenagoras, *Plea,* 18;
Justin Martyr, *1 Apology,* 3.

[9] *Commentary on Daniel,* I, 10.

[10] *On Christ and Antichrist,* 25.

empire would survive until the return of Christ to reign among men. The important point, however, is that this state would end in opposition to God. There seems to be no hint among these teachers that the government could ever become Christian.

According to Origen the state is neither Christian nor evil. Disagreeing with the Gnostics, who said that the state had no divine function and was the product of evil demons, Origen thought of government as ordained by God, but for the non-Christian world. It served a good purpose, indeed God's purpose, but because it operated through force rather than through love, it was sub-Christian. Though Christians could not participate in the civil, much less military, functions of government, the fact that they prayed, took care of the sick and wounded, and held office in God's community, the church, far outweighed any other service they could render to the state.[11]

The fathers made it very clear that even if government is not entirely just, Christians do not have the right to rebel. They insisted that rulers are responsible to God and that He will take care of them in the Judgment. There are only two hints that come even close to suggesting possible rebellion. Tertullian told the persecuting governor that if the Christians desired, they could cause a good deal of trouble to the government because they outnumbered the Romans. But this threat is stated merely hypothetically (*Apology*, 37). Origen expressly mentioned the possibility of disobedience in reaction to tyranny:

> Suppose that a man were living among the Scythians, whose laws are contrary to divine law, and he had no opportunity to go elsewhere and was compelled to live among them; such a man for the sake of true law, though illegal among the Scythians, would rightly form associations with like-minded people contrary to the laws of the Scythians. . . . For just as it would be right for people to form associations secretly to kill a tyrant who has seized control of their city, so too, since the devil, as Christians call him, and falsehood

---

11 *Against Celsus*, VIII, 73—75.

reign as tyrants, Christians form associations against the
devil . . . in order to save others.[12]

It is important to note that Origen did not give the Christians the right to rebel; indeed he expressly denounced such
a reaction (ibid., III, 15; VIII, 65). Origen felt that only
those who had not accepted the yoke of Christ, which demanded "love toward all," could engage in secret activity
against tyranny. Indeed he asserts that the non-Christians
must keep the state in order, even to the point of rebelling
against tyrants, but the Christian could not participate (ibid.,
IV, 70). Hippolytus classified sedition with fornication and
astrology as activities that excluded an individual from baptism (*Apostolic Tradition,* 16). The duty of the Christians
is obedience. Justin Martyr wrote to the emperor:

> More even than others we pay the taxes and assessments to
> those whom you appoint, as we have been taught by Him.
> For once in His time some came to Him and asked whether
> it were right to pay taxes to Caesar. And He answered . . .
> "Then give what is Caesar's to Caesar and what is God's to
> God." So we worship God only, but in other matters we
> gladly serve you, recognizing you as emperors and rulers
> of men and praying that along with your imperial power
> you may also be found to have a sound mind.[13]

Tatian felt that paying taxes was like "slavery," but he
claimed to have paid them anyway (*Oration,* 4). Tertullian
contrasted the Christians with those who were disloyal to the
emperor, and went so far as to assert: "Caesar is more ours
than yours, for our God appointed him." (*Apology,* 33)

Christians lived apart from the state as well as from pagan
society. It is important to note here, however, that this with-
drawal is not what we call "separation of church and state."
Neither the early church nor the Roman state had any con-
ception of this modern political development. As we have
already indicated, the Romans assumed that religious life
was the immediate concern of the state. There is no sug-

---

[12] *Against Celsus,* I, i. Adapted from H. Chadwick, *Origen: Contra
Celsum* (Cambridge: University Press, 1953), p. 7.

[13] *1 Apology,* 17. See Richardson, p. 253.

gestion among Christians that the state ought to be "a-religious" or that it ought to separate itself from the religious concerns of the people.

Certain statements, however, evidence a consciousness that Christians in effect were separate. Melito, bishop of Sardis in the last part of the second century, wrote to the emperor that Christianity and the Roman Empire developed together. He saw them as two separate institutions that began at the same time. Assuming that both were to serve a divine function, he suggested that they ought to work together.[14] Melito recognized in Christianity a magnitude parallel to the state and entrusted with the function of supporting the state spiritually. Origen is perhaps the best example of this type of thought. He contrasted the laws of God with those of the state (*Against Celsus,* VIII, 26). Many early fathers made this distinction, suggesting that Christians obeyed the laws of the state only when the latter were in conformity with those of God. Arguing from the fact that there were so many conflicting civil laws, they pointed out that civil legislation did not always represent the law of God. God's law, the law of nature, was the same everywhere. Human law could be evaded and was therefore imperfect. Tertullian pointed out that the pagan admitted this deficiency implicitly when certain of his laws were either repealed or no longer enforced. Divine law, Origen asserted, is never repealed and is always enforced. It is the contrast here that is important. Christians saw themselves as subjected to a law that was apart from and higher than the laws of the state. It was on this basis that they justified obeying "God rather than men." (Acts 5:29)

---

[14] Eusebius, *Eccl. Hist.,* IV, xxvi, 7—9.

APPENDIX

Readings from Primary Sources

No. 1. Teachings of the "Way of Life"

The first selection shows how the words of Jesus and of the apostles were used in the instruction of early Christians. See pp. 29—31 and 53—54. For the Didache *see p. 29 and Index.*

Didache, Chapter 1

The Lord's Teaching to the Heathen by the Twelve Apostles: There are two ways, one of life and one of death; and between the two ways there is a great difference.

Now, this is the way of life: "First, you must love God, who made you, and second, your neighbor as yourself." And whatever you want people to refrain from doing to you, you must not do to them.

What these maxims teach is this: "Bless those who curse you," and "pray for your enemies." Moreover, fast "for those who persecute you." For "what credit is it to you if you love those who love you? Is that not the way the heathen act?" But "you must love those who hate you," and then you will make no enemies. "Abstain from carnal passions." If someone strikes you "on the right cheek, turn to him the other too, and you will be perfect." If someone "forces you to go one mile with him, go along with him for two"; if someone robs you "of your overcoat, give him your suit as well." If someone deprives you of "your property, do not ask for it back." (You could not get it back anyway!) "Give to everybody who begs from you, and ask for no return." For the Father wants His own gifts to be universally shared. Happy is the man who gives as the commandment bids him, for he is guiltless! But alas for the man who receives! If he receives because he is in need, he will be guiltless. But if he is not in need, he will have to stand trial why he received and for what purpose. He will be thrown into prison and have his action investigated; and "he will not get out until he has paid back the last cent." Indeed, there is a further saying that relates to this: "Let your donation sweat in your hands until you know to whom to give it." *

Early Christian Fathers, trans. and ed. Cyril C. Richardson, *The Library of Christian Classics,* I (Philadelphia: Westminster Press, 1953), 171, 172.

No. 2. True Christian Ministers; The Sunday Assembly

The second selection from the Didache *(see p. 29) illustrates the difficulty early congregations were experiencing with itinerant Christian teachers and other traveling Christians, and the church's reaction to it (see pp. 32—39 and 43). It also contains directives about the Christian Sunday. (See pp. 31—32)*

Didache, Chapter 11

Whoever then shall come and teach you all the aforesaid, receive him. But if the teacher himself turn and teach another doctrine to destroy this, do not listen to him; but if it be to the increase of righteousness and of the knowledge of the Lord, receive him as the Lord. Now, as concerning the apostles and prophets, according to the teaching of the Gospel, so do ye; and let every apostle that cometh to you be received as the Lord; and he shall stay but one day and, if need be, the next day also; but if he stay three days, he is a false prophet. When the apostle goeth forth, let him take nothing but bread, [to suffice] till he reach his lodging; if he ask money, he is a false prophet. Ye shall not try or judge any prophet speaking in spirit. For "Every sin shall be forgiven, but this sin shall not be forgiven." But not everyone that speaketh in spirit is a prophet, but only if he have the ways of the Lord. Therefore by their ways shall be known the false prophet and the prophet.

Chapter 12

Let everyone that "cometh in the name of the Lord" be received; then, when ye have proved him, ye shall know, for ye

---

* One of the stranger "unknown sayings of Jesus," sayings which are not contained in the canonical Gospels but are quoted as words of the Lord in other early Christian writings.

can know the right hand from the left. If he that cometh be a passerby, give him all the help ye can; but he shall not stay except, if there be need, two or three days. If he wish to abide with you, being a craftsman, let him work and eat. If he have no craft, use your common sense to provide that he may live with you as a Christian, without idleness. If he be unwilling so to do, he is a "Christmonger." Beware of such.

Chapter 13

But every true prophet that willeth to abide with you is "worthy of his food." In like manner a true teacher is also, like the laborer, "worthy of his food." Therefore thou shalt take and give to the prophets every firstfruit of the produce of the winepress and the threshing floor, of oxen and sheep. For the prophets are your high priests. If ye have no prophet, give them to the poor. If thou art making a batch of bread, take the firstfruit and give according to the commandment. In like manner when thou openest a jar of wine or oil, take the firstfruit and give it to the prophets. And of money and raiment and any other possession take the firstfruit, as may seem good to thee, and give it according to the commandment.

Chapter 14

Sunday Assembly

On the Lord's day assemble and break bread and give thanks, having first confessed your sins, that your sacrifice may be pure. If any have a dispute with his fellow, let him not come to the assembly till they be reconciled, that your sacrifice be not polluted. For this is the sacrifice spoken of by the Lord: "In every place and at every time offer to Me a pure sacrifice; for I am a great King, saith the Lord, and My name is wonderful among the Gentiles." (Mal. 1:11, 14)

Chapter 15

Bishops and Deacons

Elect therefore for yourselves bishops and deacons worthy of the Lord, men that are gentle and not covetous, true men and approved; for they also minister to you the ministry of the prophets and teachers. Therefore despise them not; for these are they that are honored of you with the prophets and teachers. . . .

Documents of the Christian Church, ed. Henry Bettenson (New York & London: Oxford University Press, 1947), pp. 91—93.

No. 3. Ordination and Eucharistic Liturgy

For bishop, presbyter, and deacon, see pp. 40—46; for the celebration of Communion, see pp. 35—39. For The Apostolic Tradition, *p. 28.*

Hippolytus, The Apostolic Tradition, Chapter 2

A Bishop

Let the bishop be ordained after he has been chosen by all the people. When he has been named and shall please all, let him, with the presbytery and such bishops as may be present, assemble with the people on a Sunday. While all give their consent, the bishops shall lay their hands upon him, and the presbytery shall stand by in silence. All indeed shall keep silent, praying in their heart for the descent of the Spirit. Then one of the bishops who are present shall, at the request of all, lay his hand on him who is ordained bishop, and shall pray as follows, saying:

Chapter 3

God and Father of our Lord Jesus Christ, Father of mercies and God of all comfort, who dwellest on high yet hast respect to the lowly, who knowest all things before they come to pass. Thou hast appointed the borders of Thy church by the Word of Thy grace, predestinating from the beginning the righteous race of Abraham. And making them princes and priests, and leaving not Thy sanctuary without a ministry, Thou hast from the beginning of the world been well pleased to be glorified among those whom Thou hast chosen. Pour forth now that power, which is Thine, of Thy royal Spirit, which Thou gavest to Thy beloved Servant Jesus Christ, which He bestowed on His holy apostles, who established the church in every place, the church which Thou hast sanctified unto unceasing glory and praise of Thy name. Thou who knowest the hearts of all, grant to this Thy servant, whom Thou hast chosen to be bishop [to feed Thy holy flock] and to serve as Thy high priest without blame, ministering night and day, to propitiate Thy countenance without ceasing and to offer Thee the gifts of Thy holy church. And by the Spirit of high priesthood to have authority to remit sins according to Thy commandment, to assign the lots according to Thy precept, to loose every bond according to the authority which Thou gavest to Thy apostles, and to please Thee in meekness and purity of heart, offering to Thee an odor of sweet savor. Through Thy Servant Jesus Christ, our Lord, through whom be to Thee glory, might, honor, with [the] Holy Spirit in [the] holy church, both now and always and world without end. Amen.

Chapter 4
Eucharistic Liturgy

And when he is made bishop, all shall offer him the kiss of peace, for he has been made worthy. To him then the deacons shall bring the offering, and he, laying his hand upon it, with all the presbytery, shall say as the thanksgiving:

The Lord be with you.

And all shall say

And with thy spirit.
Lift up your hearts.
We lift them up unto the Lord.
Let us give thanks to the Lord.
It is meet and right.

And then he shall proceed immediately:

We give Thee thanks, O God, through Thy beloved Servant Jesus Christ, whom at the end of time Thou didst send to us a Savior and Redeemer and the Messenger of Thy counsel. Who is Thy Word, inseparable from Thee; through whom Thou didst make all things and in whom Thou art well pleased. Whom Thou didst send from heaven into the womb of the Virgin, and who, dwelling within her, was made flesh and was manifested as Thy Son, being born of [the] Holy Spirit and the Virgin. Who, fulfilling Thy will, and winning for Himself a holy people, spread out His hands when He came to suffer, that by His death He might set free them who believed on Thee. Who, when He was betrayed to His willing death, that He might bring to naught death, and break the bonds of the devil, and tread hell underfoot, and give light to the righteous, and set up a boundary post, and manifest His resurrection, taking bread and giving thanks to Thee said: Take, eat: this is My body, which is broken for you. And likewise also the cup, saying: This is My blood, which is shed for you. As often as ye perform this, perform My memorial.

Having in memory, therefore, His death and resurrection, we offer to Thee the bread and the cup, yielding Thee thanks, because Thou hast counted us worthy to stand before Thee and to minister to Thee.

And we pray Thee that Thou wouldest send Thy Holy Spirit upon the offerings of Thy holy church; that Thou, gathering them into one, wouldest grant to all Thy saints who partake to be filled with [the] Holy Spirit, that their faith may be confirmed in truth, that we may praise and glorify Thee. Through Thy servant Jesus Christ, through whom be to Thee glory and honor, with [the] Holy Spirit in the holy church, both now and always and world without end. Amen. . . .

Chapter 8

A Presbyter

But when a presbyter is ordained, the bishop shall lay his hand upon his head, while the presbyters touch him, and he shall say according to those things that were said above, as we have prescribed above concerning the bishop, praying and saying:

God and Father of our Lord Jesus Christ, look upon this Thy servant, and grant to him the Spirit of grace and counsel of a presbyter, that he may sustain and govern Thy people with a pure heart; as Thou didst look upon Thy chosen people and didst command Moses that he should choose presbyters, whom Thou didst fill with Thy Spirit, which Thou gavest to Thy servant. And now, O Lord, grant that there may be unfailingly preserved amongst us the Spirit of Thy grace, and make us worthy that, believing, we may minister to Thee in simplicity of heart, praising Thee. Through Thy servant Jesus Christ, through whom be to Thee glory and honor, with [the] Holy Spirit in the holy church, both now and always and world without end. Amen.

Chapter 9

A Deacon

But the deacon, when he is ordained, is chosen according to those things that were said above, the bishop alone in like manner laying his hands upon him, as we have prescribed. When the deacon is ordained, this is the reason why the bishop alone shall lay his hands upon him: he is not ordained to the priesthood but to serve the bishop and to carry out the bishop's commands. He does not take part in the council of the clergy; he is to attend to his own duties and to make known to the bishop such things as are needful. He does not receive that Spirit that is possessed by the presbytery, in which the presbyters share; he receives only what is confided in him under the bishop's authority.

For this cause the bishop alone shall make a deacon. But on a presbyter, however, the presbyters shall lay their hands because of the common and like Spirit of the clergy. Yet the presbyter has only the power to receive; but he has no power to give. For this reason a presbyter does not ordain the clergy; but at the ordination of a presbyter he seals while the bishop ordains.

Over a deacon, then, he shall say as follows:

O God, who hast created all things and hast ordered them by Thy Word, the Father of our Lord Jesus Christ, whom Thou didst send to minister Thy will and to manifest to us Thy desire, grant the Holy Spirit of grace and care and diligence to this Thy servant, whom Thou hast chosen to serve the church and to offer in Thy holy sanctuary the gifts that are offered to Thee by Thine appointed high priests . . . through Thy servant Jesus Christ, through whom be to Thee glory and honor, with the Holy Spirit in the holy church, both now and always and world without end. Amen.

The Apostolic Tradition of Hippolytus, ed. Burton Scott Easton, Archon Books (Hamden, Conn.: The Shoe String Press), pp. 33—39.

No. 4. Baptismal Creed, Immersion and Eucharist

For Baptism see pp. 28—31; for Eucharist and the Apostolic Tradition, *pp. 35—39 and 28.*

Hippolytus, Apostolic Tradition, Chapter 21

When he who is being baptized goes down into the water, he who baptizes him, putting his hand on him, shall say thus:

Dost thou believe in God, the Father Almighty?

And he who is being baptized shall say:

I believe.

Then holding his hand placed on his head, he shall baptize [immerse] him once. And then he shall say:

Dost thou believe in Christ Jesus, the Son of God, who was born of the Holy Ghost of the Virgin Mary, and was crucified under Pontius Pilate, and was dead and buried, and rose again the third day, alive from the dead, and ascended into heaven, and sat at the right hand of the Father, and will come to judge the quick and the dead? And when he says:

I believe,

he is baptized again. And again he shall say:

Dost thou believe in [the] Holy Ghost, and the holy church, and the resurrection of the flesh?

He who is being baptized shall say accordingly:

I believe,

and so he is baptized a third time. . . .

Chapter 23

And then the offering is immediately brought by the deacons to the bishop, and by thanksgiving he shall make the bread into an image of the body of Christ, and the cup of wine mixed with water according to the likeness of the blood, which is shed for all who believe in Him. And milk and honey mixed together for the fulfillment of the promise to the fathers, which spoke of a land flowing with milk and honey; namely Christ's flesh which He gave, by which they who believe are nourished like babes, He making sweet the bitter things of the heart by the gentleness of His word. And the water into an offering in a token of the laver, in order that the inner part of man, which is a living soul, may receive the same as the body.

The bishop shall explain the reason of all these things to those who partake. And when he breaks the bread and distributes the fragments he shall say:

The heavenly bread in Christ Jesus.

And the recipient shall say, Amen.

And the presbyters — or if there are not enough presbyters, the deacons — shall hold the cups . . . first he who holds the water, then the milk, thirdly the wine. And the recipients shall taste of each three times. . . .

And when these things are completed, let each one hasten to do good works . . . practicing the things he has learned, advancing in the service of God.

. . . Yet if there is any other thing that ought to be told [to converts], let the bishop impart it to them privately after their baptism; let not unbelievers know it, until they are baptized.

The Apostolic Tradition, pp. 46—49.

No. 5. Redemption Does Not Negate the Material World

Irenaeus (see pp. 57—60) wrote his Against All Heresies *to combat Gnosticism (see pp. 54—56). In the following selection Irenaeus shows that the material world must be of God if God wills to use bread and wine through which to give His body and blood. Such Eucharist is according to Irenaeus the kind of sacrifice that God desires.*

Book IV, Chapter XVIII

4. Inasmuch, then, as the church offers with single-mindedness, her gift is justly reckoned a pure sacrifice with God. As Paul also says to the Philippians, "I am full, having received from Epaphroditus the things that were sent from you, the odor of a sweet smell, a sacrifice acceptable, pleasing to God." For it behooves us to make an oblation to God, and in all things to be found grateful to God our Maker, in a pure mind, and in faith without hypocrisy, in well-grounded hope, in fervent love, offering the firstfruits of His own created things. And the church alone offers this pure oblation to the Creator, offering to Him, with giving of thanks, [the things taken] from His creation. But the Jews do not offer thus: for their hands are full of blood; for they have not received the Word, through whom it is offered to God. Nor, again, do any of the conventicles *(synagogae)* of the heretics [offer this]. For some, by maintaining that the Father is different from the Creator, do, when they offer to Him what belongs to this creation of ours, set Him forth as being covetous of another's property, and desirous of what is not His own. Those, again, who maintain that the things around us originated from apostasy, ignorance, and passion, do, while offering unto Him the fruits of ignorance, passion, and apostasy, sin against their Father, rather subjecting Him to insult than giving Him thanks. But how can they be

consistent with themselves, [when they say] that the bread over which thanks have been given is the body of their Lord, and the cup His blood, if they do not call Himself the Son of the Creator of the world, that is, His Word, through whom the wood fructifies, and the fountains gush forth, and the earth gives "first the blade, then the ear, then the full corn in the ear"?

5. Then, again, how can they say that the flesh, which is nourished with the body of the Lord and with His blood, goes to corruption, and does not partake of life? Let them, therefore, either alter their opinion or cease from offering the things just mentioned. But our opinion is in accordance with the Eucharist, and the Eucharist in turn establishes our opinion. For we offer to Him His own, announcing consistently the fellowship and union of the flesh and Spirit. For as the bread, which is produced from the earth, when it receives the invocation of God is no longer common bread, but the Eucharist, consisting of two realities, earthly and heavenly, so also our bodies, when they receive the Eucharist, are no longer corruptible, having the hope of the resurrection to eternity.

The Ante-Nicene Fathers, Vol. I, eds. Alexander Roberts and James Donaldson (Grand Rapids: Wm. B. Eerdmans Publishing Company, 1950), 485, 486.

No. 6. Called to a Different Way of Life

The following is from what appears to be a sermon (see pp. 31; 32—34) from the second century. It is a good illustration of early Christian interpretation of the Scriptures and of the Christian life (see pp. 70—78). It was evidently bound together with a letter written by Clement of Rome (see p. 41 of the text) and so was for many centuries taken as another letter by him. Hence its name Second [letter of] Clement.

2 Clement, Chapter 1

Brothers, we ought to think of Jesus Christ as we do of God — as the "judge of the living and the dead." And we ought not to belittle our salvation. For when we belittle Him, we hope to get but little; and they that listen as to a trifling matter do wrong. And we too do wrong when we fail to realize whence and by whom and into what circumstances we were called, and how much suffering Jesus Christ endured for us. How, then, shall we repay Him, or what return is worthy of His gift to us? How many blessings we owe to Him! For He has given us light; as a Father He has called us sons; He has rescued us when we were perishing. How, then, shall we praise Him, or how repay Him for what we have received? Our minds were impaired; we worshiped stone and wood and gold and silver and brass, the works of men; and our whole life was nothing else but death. So when we were wrapped in darkness and our eyes were full of such mist, by His will we recovered our sight and put off the cloud which infolded us. For He took pity on us and in His tenderness saved us, since He saw our great error and ruin, and that we had no hope of salvation unless it came from Him. For He called us when we were nothing, and willed our existence from nothing.

Chapter 2

"Rejoice, you who are barren and childless; cry out and shout, you who were never in labor; for the desolate woman has many more children than the one with the husband."

When he says, "Rejoice, you who are barren and childless," he refers to us; for our church was barren before it was given children. And when he says, "Shout, you who were never in labor," this is what he means: we should offer our prayers to God with sincerity, and not lose heart like women in labor. And he says, "The desolate woman has many more children than the one with the husband," because our people seemed to be abandoned by God. But now that we believe, we have become more numerous than those who seemed to have God. And another Scripture says, "I did not come to call the righteous, but sinners." This means that those perishing must be saved. Yes, a great and wonderful thing it is to support, not things which are standing, but those which are collapsing. Thus it was that the Christ willed to save what was perishing; and He saved many when He came and called us who were actually perishing. . . .

Chapter 5

Therefore, brothers, ceasing to tarry in this world, let us do the will of Him who called us, and let us not be afraid to leave this world. For the Lord said, "You will be like lambs among wolves." But Peter replied by saying, "What if the wolves tear the lambs to pieces?" Jesus said to Peter: "After their death the lambs should not fear the wolves, nor should you fear those who kill you and can do nothing more to you. But fear Him who, when you are dead, has power over soul and body to cast them into the flames of hell." You must realize, brothers, that our stay in this world of the flesh is slight and short, but Christ's promise is great and wonderful, and means rest in the coming Kingdom and in eternal life. What, then, must we do to get these things, except to lead a holy and upright life and to regard these things of the world as alien to us and not to desire them? For in wanting to obtain these things we fall from the right way.

Chapter 6

The Lord says, "No servant can serve two masters." If we want to serve both God and money, it will do us no good. "For what good does it do a man to gain the whole world and forfeit his life?" This world and the world to come are two enemies. This one means adultery, corruption, avarice, and deceit, while the other gives them up. We cannot, then, be friends of both. To get the one, we must give the other up. We think that it is better to hate what is here, for it is trifling, transitory, and perishable, and to value what is there — things good and imperishable. Yes, if we do the will of Christ, we shall find rest, but if not, nothing will save us from eternal punishment, if we fail to heed His commands. Furthermore, the Scripture also says in Ezekiel, "Though Noah and Job and Daniel should rise, they shall not save their children in captivity." If even such upright men as these cannot save their children by their uprightness, what assurance have we that we shall enter God's kingdom if we fail to keep our baptism pure and undefiled? Or who will plead for us if we are not found to have holy and upright deeds? . . .

Chapter 14

So, my brothers, by doing the will of God our Father we shall belong to the first church, the spiritual one, which was created before the sun and the moon. But if we fail to do the Lord's will, that passage of Scripture will apply to us which says, "My house has become a robbers' den." So, then, we must choose to belong to the church of life in order to be saved. I do not suppose that you are ignorant that the living "church is the body of Christ." For Scripture says, "God made man male and female." The male is Christ; the female is the church. The Bible, moreover, and the apostles say that the church is not limited to the present, but existed from the beginning. For it was spiritual, as was our Jesus, and was made manifest in the last days to save us. Indeed, the church, which is spiritual, was made manifest in the flesh of Christ, and so indicates to us that if any of us guard it in the flesh and do not corrupt it, he will get it in return by the Holy Spirit. For this flesh is the antitype* of the spirit. Consequently, no one who has corrupted the antitype will share in the reality. This, then, is what it means, brothers: Guard the flesh so that you may share in the spirit. Now, if we say that the church is the flesh and the Christ is the spirit, then he who does violence to the flesh does violence to the church.

Such a person, then, will not share in the spirit, which is Christ. This flesh is able to share in so great a life and immortality, because the Holy Spirit cleaves to it. Nor can one express or tell "what things the Lord has prepared" for His chosen ones. . . .

Chapter 16

So, brothers, since we have been given no small opportunity to repent, let us take the occasion to turn to God who has called us, while we still have One to accept us. For if we renounce these pleasures and master our souls by avoiding their evil lusts, we shall share in Jesus' mercy. Understand that "the day" of judgment is already "on its way like a furnace ablaze," and "the powers of heaven will dissolve" and the whole earth will be like lead melting in fire. Then men's secret and overt actions will be made clear. Charity, then, like repentance from sin, is a good thing. But fasting is better than prayer, and charity than both. "Love covers a multitude of sins," and prayer, arising from a good conscience, "rescues from death." Blessed is everyone who abounds in these things, for charity lightens sin. . . .

Chapter 19

So, my brothers and sisters, after God's truth I am reading you an exhortation to heed what was there written, so that

* *Something which foreshadows the "type" which will correspond to it.*

you may save yourselves and your reader. For compensation
I beg you to repent with all your heart, granting yourselves salvation and life. By doing this we will set a goal for all the
young who want to be active in the cause of religion and of
God's goodness. We should not, moreover, be so stupid as to
be displeased and vexed when anyone admonishes us and converts us from wickedness to righteousness. There are times
when we do wrong unconsciously because of the double-minded-
ness and unbelief in our hearts, and "our understanding is
darkened" by empty desires. Let us, then, do what is right so
that we may finally be saved. Blessed are they who observe
these injunctions; though they suffer briefly in this world, they
will gather the immortal fruit of the resurrection. . . .
Early Christian Fathers, pp. 193—195; 198—201.

No. 7. Restoration of Fallen Members

*For the public repentance of "lapsed" Christians, or the "sec-
ond (i. e., postbaptismal) repentance," see pp. 72—74. The
reading is from a work by the African writer Tertullian
(c. 160—c. 220).*

On Penitence, Chapter 7

Grant, Lord Christ, that Thy servants may speak of the
discipline of penitence, or hear of it, only while the duty of
avoiding sin rests on them as catechumens. In other words, may
they thereafter know nothing of repentance nor have any need
of it. I am reluctant to make mention here of a second hope,
one which is indeed the very last, for fear that in treating of
a resource which yet remains in penitence, I may seem to
indicate that there is still time left for sin. God grant that no
one come to such a conclusion, as though the road still lay
open before him for sin because it still lies open for penitence
and as though he were free to find in the superabundance of
heavenly mercy justification for the excesses of human presumption. Let no one be worse because God is better, sinning
just as often as he is forgiven. Otherwise, while there will be
no end to his sin, there will be, of a certainty, an end to his
immunity.

We have escaped once. Let us not place ourselves in danger
again, even though it seems that we shall again escape. Most
men who are saved from shipwreck divorce both ship and sea
from that time on. . . .

But that stubborn enemy of ours never gives his wickedness a rest. Rather he is then most furious when he sees that a man is completely free; then he is most on fire when he is quenched. He must needs grieve and groan that, when pardon is granted for sins, so many works of death in man are mastered, so many titles of his former dominion are erased. He grieves that the sinner, the servant of Christ, is to judge him and his angels. Therefore he watches, he attacks, he lays siege, in the hope that by some means or other he may be able to strike at his eyes with concupiscence of the flesh or entangle his soul in worldly delights or destroy his faith through a fear of the civil authorities or bring him to deviate from the right way by perverted doctrines. Never is he at a loss for stumbling blocks or temptations.

Accordingly, since God foresees this virulence of his, He has permitted the door of forgiveness, although it is closed and locked by the bar of Baptism, still to stand somewhat open. He has placed in the vestibule a second penitence so that it may open the door to those who knock; only once, however, because it is already a second time; never again, however, because the last time was in vain. For is not even this "once" enough? You have what you no longer deserved, since you lost what you had received. If the indulgence of the Lord favors you with what you need for the restoration of that which you lost, be grateful for His repeated, nay rather, for His increased beneficence. For to give back is a greater thing than to give, since it is worse to have lost than never to have received at all.

But if a man is obliged to a second penitence, his spirit must not be cast down and crushed by despair. Of course, he should be reluctant to sin again, but to repent again he should not be reluctant. He should be ashamed to place himself again in danger, but to be saved again no one should be ashamed. When a disease recurs the medicine must be repeated. You will prove your gratitude to the Lord, if you do not refuse what He offers you anew. You have sinned, yet you can still be reconciled. You have someone to whom you can make satisfaction, yes, and one who wills it.

Chapter 9

Since this second and last penitence is so serious a matter, it must be tested in a way which is proportionately laborious. Therefore it must not be performed solely within one's conscience but it must also be shown forth in some external act. This external act, rather expressively designated by the Greek word for it in common use, is the *exomologesis* [confession]. Herein we confess our sin to the Lord, not as though He were ignorant of it, but because satisfaction receives its proper determination through confession, confession gives birth to penitence, and by penitence God is appeased. . . .

Chapter 10

Where there are two together, there is the church — and the church is Christ. When, therefore, you stretch forth your hands to the knees of the brethren, you are in touch with Christ and you win the favor of Christ by your supplications. In like manner, when they shed tears for you, it is Christ who suffers, Christ who supplicates the Father. And what the Son requests is always easily obtained. . . .

Tertullian, *On Penance and on Purity*, trans. William P. Le Saint, *Ancient Christian Writers*, XXVIII (Westminster, Md.: The Newman Press, 1959), 27—29, 31, 33.

No. 8. The Christian Defense: The Moral Quality of Christians

Early Christian apologists (pp. 92—93) describe the moral life of the Christians as superior to that of the Romans. This was necessary because the Romans accused the Christians of immoralities. The apologias give us a glimpse of the transformation of lives and attitudes which the Gospel effected. See pp. 75—85. For the apologist Justin see p. 28 and Appendix, pp. 123—125.

Justin, First Apology, Chapter 11

When you hear that we look for a kingdom, you rashly suppose that we mean something merely human. But we speak of a kingdom with God, as is clear from our confessing Christ when you bring us to trial, though we know that death is the penalty for this confession. For if we looked for a human kingdom we would deny it in order to save our lives, and would try to remain in hiding in order to obtain the things we look for. But since we do not place our hopes on the present [order], we are not troubled by being put to death, since we will have to die somehow in any case.

Chapter 12

We are in fact of all men your best helpers and allies in securing good order, convinced as we are that no wicked man, no covetous man or conspirator, or virtuous man either, can be hidden from God and that everyone goes to eternal punishment or salvation in accordance with the character of his actions. If all men knew this, nobody would choose vice even for a little time, knowing that he was on his way to eternal punishment by fire; every man would follow the self-restrained and orderly path of virtue, so as to receive the good things that come from God and avoid His punishments. There are some who merely try to conceal their wrongdoings because of the laws and punishments which you decree, knowing that since you are only men it is possible for wrongdoers to escape you; if they learned and were convinced that our thoughts as well as our actions cannot be hidden from God they would certainly lead orderly lives, if only because of the consequences, as you must agree. But it seems as if you were afraid of having all men well-behaved, and nobody left for you to punish; this would be the conduct of public executioners, not of good rulers. Such things, we are convinced, are brought about by the evil demons, the ones who demand sacrifices and service from men who live irrationally; but we have not learned [to expect] any unreasonable conduct from you, who aim at piety and philosophy. But if like thoughtless men you prefer custom to truth, then go ahead and do what you can. Rulers who respect reputation rather than truth have as much power as brigands in a desert.

Chapter 14

. . . Those who once rejoiced in fornication now delight in continence alone; those who made use of magic arts have dedicated themselves to the good and unbegotten God; we who once took most pleasure in the means of increasing our wealth and property now bring what we have into a common fund and share with everyone in need; we who hated and killed one another and would not associate with men of different tribes because of [their different] customs now after the manifestation of Christ live together and pray for our enemies and try to persuade those who unjustly hate us, so that they, living according to the fair commands of Christ, may share with us the good hope of receiving the same things [that we will] from God, the Master of all.

The following description of the quality of the Christian life is from an anonymous early-second-century apologia written as a letter to a distinguished Roman.

Letter to Diognetus, Chapter 5

. . . Yet, although they live in Greek and barbarian cities alike, as each man's lot has been cast, and follow the customs of the country in clothing and food and other matters of daily living, at the same time they give proof of the remarkable and admittedly extraordinary constitution of their own commonwealth. They live in their own countries, but only as aliens. They have a share in every thing as citizens, and endure everything as foreigners. Every foreign land is their fatherland, and yet for them every fatherland is a foreign land. They marry, like everyone else, and they beget children, but they do not cast out their offspring. They share their board with each other, but not their marriage bed. It is true that they are "in the flesh," but they do not live "according to the flesh." They busy themselves on earth, but their citizenship is in heaven. They obey the established laws, but in their own lives they go far beyond what the laws require. They love all men, and by all men are persecuted. They are unknown, and still they are condemned; they are put to death, and yet they are brought to life. They are poor, and yet they make many rich; they are completely destitute, and yet they enjoy complete abundance. They are dishonored, and in their very dishonor are glorified; they are defamed, and are vindicated. They are reviled, and yet they bless; when they are affronted, they still pay due respect. When they do good, they are punished as evildoers; undergoing punishment, they rejoice because they are brought to life. They are treated by the Jews as foreigners and enemies, and are hunted down by the Greeks; and all the time those who hate them find it impossible to justify their enmity.

Chapter 6

To put it simply: What the soul is in the body, that Christians are in the world. The soul is dispersed through all the members of the body, and Christians are scattered through all the cities of the world. The soul dwells in the body, but does not belong to the body, and Christians dwell in the world, but do not belong to the world. The soul, which is invisible, is kept under guard in the visible body; in the same way, Christians are recognized when they are in the world, but their religion remains unseen. The flesh hates the soul and treats it as an enemy, even though it has suffered no wrong, because it is prevented from enjoying its pleasures; so too the world hates Christians, even though it suffers no wrong at their hands, because they range themselves against its pleasures. The soul loves the flesh that hates it, and its members; in the same way, Christians love those who hate them. The soul is shut up in the body, and yet itself holds the body together; while Christians are restrained in the world as in a prison, and yet themselves hold the world together. The soul, which is immortal, is housed in a mortal dwelling; while Christians are settled among corruptible things, to wait for the incorruptibility that will be theirs in heaven. The soul, when faring badly as to food and drink, grows better; so too Christians, when punished, day by day increase more and more. It is to no less a post than this that God has ordered them, and they must not try to evade it.

Early Christian Fathers, pp. 217, 218, 247—249.

No. 9. The Persecution of Christians

One of the most characteristic aspects of early Christian history was the ever-present possibility of martyrdom (see pp. 88 to 92). We have good descriptions of what this involved from as early as the first and early second centuries. The pagan writer Tacitus (55?—c.117) in his Annales *describes how the Christians were treated by Nero.*

Annales, Chapter XV, 44

But all the endeavors of men, all the emperor's largesse and the propitiations of the gods, did not suffice to allay the scandal or banish the belief that the fire had been ordered. And so, to get rid of this rumor, Nero set up as the culprits and punished with the utmost refinement of cruelty a class hated for their abominations, who are commonly called Christians. Christus, from whom their name is derived, was executed at the hands of the procurator Pontius Pilate in the reign of Tiberius.

Checked for the moment, this pernicious superstition again broke out, not only in Judaea, the source of the evil, but even in Rome, that receptacle for everything that is sordid and degrading from every quarter of the globe, which there finds a following. Accordingly, arrest was first made of those who confessed [sc. *to being Christians*]; then, on their evidence, an immense multitude was convicted, not so much on the charge of arson as because of hatred of the human race. Besides being put to death they were made to serve as objects of amusement; they were clad in the hides of beasts and torn to death by dogs; others were crucified, others set on fire to serve to illuminate the night when daylight failed. Nero had thrown open his grounds for the display, and was putting on a show in the circus, where he mingled with the people in the dress of charioteer or drove about in his chariot. All this gave rise to a feeling of pity, even towards men whose guilt merited the most exemplary punishment; for it was felt that they were being destroyed not for the public good but to gratify the cruelty of an individual.

Pliny's letter to the Emperor Trajan, c. 112 A.D. (see p. 31), describes the difficulties that many Roman governors felt in carrying out the persecution policy.

Letters, X, 96

It is my rule, Sire, to refer to you in matters where I am uncertain. For who can better direct my hesitation or instruct my ignorance? I was never present at any trial of Christians; therefore I do not know what are the customary penalties or investigations, and what limits are observed. I have hesitated a great deal on the question whether there should be any distinction of ages; whether the weak should have the same treatment as the more robust; whether those who recant should be pardoned, or whether a man who has ever been a Christian should gain nothing by ceasing to be such; whether the name itself, even if innocent of crime, should be punished, or only the crimes attaching to that name.

Meanwhile, this is the course that I have adopted in the case of those brought before me as Christians. I ask them if they are Christians. If they admit it I repeat the question a second and a third time, threatening capital punishment; if they persist I sentence them to death. For I do not doubt that, whatever kind of crime it may be to which they have confessed, their pertinacity and inflexible obstinacy should certainly be punished. There were others who displayed a like madness and whom I reserved to be sent to Rome, since they were Roman citizens.

Thereupon the usual result followed; the very fact of my dealing with the question led to a wider spread of the charge, and a great variety of cases were brought before me. An anonymous pamphlet was issued, containing many names. All who denied that they were or had been Christians I considered should be discharged, because they called upon the gods at my dictation and did reverence, with incense and wine, to your image which I had ordered to be brought forward for this purpose, together with the statues of the deities; and especially because they cursed Christ, a thing which, it is said, genuine Christians cannot be induced to do. Others named by the informer first said that they were Christians and then denied it; declaring that they had been but were so no longer, some having recanted three years or more before and one or two as long ago as 20 years. They all worshiped your image and the statues of the gods and cursed Christ.

But they declared that the sum of their guilt or error had amounted only to this, that on an appointed day they had been accustomed to meet before daybreak, and to recite a hymn antiphonally to Christ, as to a god, and to bind themselves by an oath, not for the commission of any crime but to abstain from theft, robbery, adultery, and breach of faith, and not to deny a deposit when it was claimed. After the conclusion of this ceremony it was their custom to depart and meet again to take food; but it was ordinary and harmless food, and they had ceased this practice after my edict in which, in accordance with your orders, I had forbidden secret societies. I thought it the more necessary, therefore, to find out what truth there was in this by applying torture to two maidservants, who were called deaconesses. But I found nothing but a depraved and extravagant superstition, and I therefore postponed my examination and had recourse to you for consultation.

The matter seemed to me to justify my consulting you, especially on account of the number of those imperiled; for many persons of all ages and classes and of both sexes are being put in peril by accusation, and this will go on. The contagion of this superstition has spread not only in the cities, but in the villages and rural districts as well; yet it seems capable of being checked and set right. There is no shadow of doubt that the temples, which have been almost deserted, are beginning to be frequented once more, that the sacred rites which have been long neglected are being renewed, and that sacrificial victims are for sale everywhere, whereas, till recently, a buyer was rarely to be found. From this it is easy to imagine what a host of men could be set right, were they given a chance of recantation."

Trajan's reply explained the imperial policy towards Christians.

Letters, X, 97

You have taken the right line, my dear Pliny, in examining the cases of those denounced to you as Christians, for no hard and fast rule can be laid down, of universal application. They are not to be sought out; if they are informed against, and the charge is proved, they are to be punished, with this reservation — that if anyone denies that he is a Christian, and actually proves it, that is by worshiping our gods, he shall be pardoned as a result of his recantation, however suspect he may have been with respect to the past. Pamphlets published anonymously should carry no weight in any charge whatsoever. They constitute a very bad precedent, and are also out of keeping with this age.

Many Christians died for their faith. The records of some of these executions have been preserved. They were kept by congregations for devotional use and to encourage members facing persecution. The following account of their bishop's heroic death in 155 (see p. 90) was circulated as a letter of the church of Smyrna.

The Martyrdom of Polycarp

III. . . . All the crowd, astonished at the noble conduct of the God-beloved and God-fearing race of Christians, cried out, "Away with the atheists [those who will not worship the gods]; let search be made for Polycarp."

V. But the most admirable Polycarp when first he heard of this was not dismayed, but wished to remain in the city. The majority, however, prevailed on him to withdraw. And he withdrew to a small estate not far from the city. There he passed the time with a few companions, wholly occupied night and day

in prayer for all men and for the churches throughout the world;
as, indeed, was his habit. And while at prayer he fell into
a trance three days before his arrest and saw his pillow set on
fire. And he turned and said to his companions, "I must needs
be burned alive."

VI. Now since they that sought him were persistent, he departed to another estate. Then straightway they were upon him,
and when they did not find him they apprehended two young
servants. Of whom one confessed under torture; for it was
impossible for him to escape since they that betrayed him were
of his own household. Then the sheriff, who bore by God's
appointment the same name [sc. as our Lord's judge], being
called Herod, hastened to bring him into the stadium, that he
might fulfill his own appointed lot by becoming a partner of
Christ, and that his betrayers might undergo the punishment
of Judas himself.

VII. So, on the day of the preparation, mounted police with
their usual arms set out about supper time, taking with them
the servant, hurrying "as against a thief." And at a late hour
they came up to the place and found him in a cottage, lying
in an upper room. He could have gone away to another farm,
but he would not, saying, "The will of God be done." So, hearing their arrival, he came down and talked with them, while
all that were present marveled at his age and constancy, and
that there was so much ado about the arrest of such an old man.
Then he ordered that something should be served for them to
eat and drink, at that late hour, as much as they wanted. And
he besought them that they should grant him an hour that he
might pray freely. They gave him leave, and he stood and
prayed, being so filled with the grace of God that for two
hours he could not hold his peace, while they that heard were
amazed, and the men repented that they had come after so
venerable an old man.

VIII. When he had brought to an end his prayer, in which
he made mention of all, small and great, high and low, with
whom he had had dealings, and of the whole catholic church
throughout the world, the time had come for him to depart. And
they set him on an ass and led him into the city. Now it was
a high Sabbath. And there met him the sheriff Herod, and his
father Nicetes, who removed him into their carriage, and tried
to persuade him, sitting by his side and saying, "Now what

harm is there in saying 'Lord Caesar,' and in offering incense, and so on, and thus saving thyself?" He at first made no reply, but since they persisted he said, "I do not intend to do what you advise." Then, failing to persuade him, they began to use threatening words; and they pulled him down hastily, so that he grazed his shin as he descended from the carriage. Without turning back, as if he had suffered no hurt, he went on with all speed, and was led to the stadium, wherein the tumult was so great that no one could be heard.

IX. Now, as he was entering the stadium, there came to Polycarp a voice from heaven, "Be strong, Polycarp, and play the man." And no one saw the speaker, but the voice was heard by those of our people who were there. Thereupon he was led forth, and great was the uproar of them that heard that Polycarp had been seized. Accordingly, he was led before the Proconsul, who asked him if he were the man himself. And when he confessed the Proconsul tried to persuade him, saying, "Have respect to thine age," and so forth, according to their customary form; "Swear by the genius of Caesar," "Repent," "Say, 'Away with the atheists!' " Then Polycarp looked with a severe countenance on the mob of lawless heathen in the stadium, and he waved his hand at them, and looking up to heaven he groaned and said, "Away with the atheists!" But the Proconsul urged him and said, "Swear, and I will release thee; curse the Christ." And Polycarp said, "Eighty and six years have I served Him, and He hath done me no wrong; how then can I blaspheme my King who saved me?"

X. But the Proconsul again persisted and said, "Swear by the genius of Caesar"; and he answered, "If thou dost vainly imagine that I would swear by the genius of Caesar, as thou sayest, pretending not to know what I am, hear plainly that I am a Christian. And if thou art willing to learn the doctrine of Christianity, grant me a day and hearken to me." Then said the Proconsul, "Persuade the people." Polycarp replied, "Thee I had deemed worthy of discourse, for we are taught to render to authorities and the powers ordained of God honor as is fitting. But I deem not this mob worthy that I should defend myself before them."

XI. Then said the Proconsul, "I have wild beasts; if thou repent not, I will throw thee to them." But he said, "Send for them. For repentance from better to worse is not a change permitted to us; but to change from cruelty to righteousness is a noble thing." Then said the Proconsul again, "If thou dost despise the wild beasts I will make thee to be consumed by fire, if thou repent not." And Polycarp answered, "Thou threatenest the fire that burns for an hour and in a little while is quenched; for thou knowest not of the fire of the judgment to come, and the fire of the eternal punishment, reserved for the ungodly. But why delayest thou? Bring what thou wilt."

XII. As he spake these words and many more, he was filled with courage and joy; and his countenance was full of grace, so that not only did it fall not in dismay at what was being said to him, but on the contrary the Proconsul was astonished, and sent his herald to proclaim thrice in the midst of the stadium, "Polycarp hath confessed himself to be a Christian." When this was proclaimed by the herald the whole multitude of Gentiles and Jews who dwelt in Smyrna cried out with ungovernable rage and in a loud voice, "This is the teacher of Asia, the father of the Christians, the destroyer of our gods, that teacheth many not to sacrifice nor worship." They kept shouting this, asking Philip, the Asiarch, to loose a lion at Polycarp. But he said that it was not lawful for him, since he had finished the sports. Then they decided to shout with one accord that he should be burned alive. For the matter of his vision of the pillow must needs be fulfilled, when he saw it burning while he was at prayer, and turned and said prophetically to his companions, "I must needs be burned alive."

XIII. And now things happened with such speed, in less time than it takes to tell; for the mob straightway brought together timber and faggots from the workshops and baths, the Jews giving themselves zealously to the work, as they were like to do. . . . They were about to nail him to the stake, when he said, "Let me be as I am. He that granted me to endure the fire will grant me also to remain at the pyre unmoved, without being secured with nails."

XV. When he had ended his prayer the firemen lighted the fire. And a great flame flashed forth; and we, to whom it was given to see, beheld a marvel. . . . The fire took the shape of a vault, like a ship's sail bellying in the wind, and it made a wall round the martyr's body; and there was the body in the midst, like a loaf being baked or like gold and silver being tried in the furnace. . . .

XVI. So at length the lawless ones, seeing that his body could not be consumed by the fire, bade an executioner approach him to drive in a dagger. And when he had done this there came out . . . abundance of blood so that it quenched the fire, and all the multitude marveled at the great difference between the unbelievers and the elect. . . ."

Documents of the Christian Church, selected and edited by Henry Bettenson (New York & London: Oxford University Press, 1947), pp. 3—7, 13—17.

The Christian teacher and philosopher Justin (see pp. 28; 36; Appendix, 113) was brought to his death by the philosopher Crescens, whom Justin had defeated in a philosophical debate. Justin was tried and executed with six other Christians — one a woman, one a slave, and a bystander at the trial who volunteered his confession. The following gives what seems a first-hand report on the cross-examination of Christians in court.

Acts of SS. Justin and His Companions

II. . . . Brought before the judgment seat, Justin was addressed by Rusticus the prefect: "First of all obey the gods, and make submission to the Princes."

Justin said: "To obey the commands of our Savior Jesus Christ is not worthy of blame or condemnation."

The prefect Rusticus said: "What doctrines do you hold?"

Justin said: "I have endeavored to make myself acquainted with all doctrines, but I have given my assent to the true doctrines of the Christians, whether they please the holders of false beliefs or no."

The prefect Rusticus said: "Do those doctrines please you, you wretch?"

Justin said: "Yes, for the belief in accordance with which I follow them is right."

The prefect Rusticus said: "What belief do you mean?"

Justin said: "That which we religiously profess concerning the God of the Christians, in whom we believe, one God, existing from the beginning, Maker and Artificer of the whole creation, seen and unseen; and concerning our Lord Jesus Christ, the Son of God, who has also been proclaimed aforetime by the prophets as about to come to the race of men for herald of salvation and for master of true disciples. And I, being but a man, regard what I say to be of little worth in comparison of His infinite Godhead, but there is a power in prophecy, and that I acknowledge; therein hath proclamation been made aforetime of Him of whom I just spoke as the Son of God. For I know that from the beginning the prophets foretold His coming among men."

III. The prefect Rusticus said: "Where do you meet together?"

Justin said: "Where each wills and can. Do you really think that we all meet in the same place? Not so: for the God of the Christians is not confined by place, but being unseen fills heaven and earth, and is worshiped and glorified by the faithful everywhere."

The prefect Rusticus said: "Tell me, where do ye meet, or in what place do you gather your disciples?"

Justin said: "I lodge above in the house of Martin, near the baths of Timothy, and during all this time (this is my second visit to Rome) I have known no other place of meeting but his house. And if any wished to come to me, I imparted to him the word of truth."

Rusticus said: "To come to the point then, are you a Christian?"

Justin said: "Yes, I am a Christian."

IV. . . . Rusticus said to Euelpistus: "And what are you?"

Euelpistus, a slave of Caesar, answered: "I am also a Christian, freed by Christ, and share by the grace of Christ in the same hope."

The prefect Rusticus said to Hierax: "Are you also a Christian?"

Hierax said: "Yes, I am a Christian, for I worship and adore the same God."

The prefect Rusticus said: "Did Justin make you Christians?"

Hierax said: "I was, and shall ever be, a Christian."

A man called Paeon stood up and said: "I also am a Christian."

The prefect Rusticus said: "Who taught you?"

Paeon said: "I received from my parents this good confession."

Euelpistus said: "I listened indeed gladly to the words of Justin, but I too received Christianity from my parents."

The prefect Rusticus said: "Where are your parents?"

Euelpistus said: "In Cappadocia."

Rusticus said to Hierax: "Where are your parents?"

He answered, saying: "Our true father is Christ, and our mother our faith in Him. My earthly parents are dead, and I was dragged away from Iconium in Phrygia before coming hither. . . ."

V. The prefect said to Justin: "Listen, you that are said to be a learned man, and think that you are acquainted with true doctrine, if you shall be scourged and beheaded, are you persuaded that you will ascend to heaven?"

Justin said: "I hope to have His gifts if I endure these things. For I know that for all who live so, there abides until the consummation of the whole world the free gift of God."

The prefect Rusticus said: "Do you then think that you will ascend to heaven, to receive certain rewards?"

Justin said: "I do not think, I know and am fully persuaded."

The prefect Rusticus said: "Let us now come to the pressing matter in hand. Agree together and sacrifice with one accord to the gods."

Justin said: "No one who is rightly minded turns from true belief to false."

The prefect Rusticus said: "If you do not obey, you shall be punished without mercy."

Justin said: "If we are punished for the sake of our Lord Jesus Christ we hope to be saved, for this shall be our salvation and confidence before the more terrible judgment seat of our Lord and Savior, who shall judge the whole world." So also said the other martyrs: "Do what you will. For we are Christians and offer no sacrifice to idols."

Rusticus the prefect gave sentence: "Let those who will not sacrifice to the gods and yield to the command of the Emperor be scourged and led away to be beheaded in accordance with the laws."

VI. The holy martyrs went out glorifying God to the customary place and were beheaded, and fulfilled their testimony by the confession of their Savior. And some of the faithful took their bodies by stealth and laid them in a convenient place, the grace of our Lord Jesus Christ working with them, to whom be glory for ever and ever. Amen.

E. C. E. Owen, *Some Authentic Acts of the Early Martyrs* (London: SPCK, 1933), very slightly altered.

Suggestions for Further Reading

A fine introduction to early Christianity and later Christian history is that by Williston Walker, *A History of the Christian Church,* revised (New York: Charles Scribner's Sons, 1959). More interpretive is the incisive treatment by Martin E. Marty, *A Short History of Christianity* (A Living Age Book, paperback, published by Meridian, 1959). There is an excellent collection of maps and other introductory material, including many photographs of archaeological remains with the art of the period, in the *Atlas of the Early Christian World.* (London: Thomas Nelson and Sons Ltd., 1958)

There are many editions of the early church fathers in English. Among the most recent ones are the first six volumes of *The Library of Christian Classics,* edited by John Baillie et al (Philadelphia: Westminster Press, and the *Ancient Christian Writers* series (Westminster, Md.: The Newman Press). The first five volumes of the *Ante-Nicene Fathers* series, republished from the edition of 1896 (Grand Rapids: Eerdmans, 1952), are old now but still useful. Edgar Goodspeed's edition of the *Apostolic Fathers* (New York: Harper, 1950) is perhaps the most readable. Two available collections of documents, Roland Bainton's paperback, *Early Christianity* (Princeton: D. Van Nostrand, 1960), and Henry Bettenson's *Documents of the Christian Church* (New York: Oxford Univ. Press, 1947), will also prove helpful. Hippolytus' *Apostolic Tradition* is available in an edition edited by Burton S. Easton. (Hamden, Conn.: Shoe String Press, Archon Books, 1962)

The stories of the martyrs have been conveniently collected by E. C. Owen in *Some Authentic Acts of the Early*

Martyrs (London: SPCK, 1933). Oscar Cullman's *Peter* (New York: Meridian Living Age Book, paperback, 1958) is an interesting presentation of the foundations of the papacy, and Joachim Jeremias' *Infant Baptism in the First Four Centuries* (Philadelphia: Westminster Press, 1960) gives a fair evaluation of the evidence.

Index

Presbyter[s], [-y] 19, 20, 22,
30, 40—43, 44, 48, 49,
102, 103—104, 105; *see
also* Bishop; Ministry;
Sacerdotalism
Proselytes 16—17, 31
Recapitulation theory 58—60
Repentance, public 72—73,
111—113; *see also* Sin
and forgiveness
Rules of faith 56—57
Sacerdotalism 45—46, 47; *see
also* Bishop; Deacon;
Ministry; Presbyter
Scripture[s] 36, 42, 53—54,
99, 109, 109—110
apocryphal 33, 53—54, 55
interpretation of 107
lessons 31, 32—35, 99
loyalty to 63—64
New Testament 11, 27, 31,
40, 56
Acts 11, 33, 38, 53, 57
Epistles 11, 53
Gospels 11, 23, 33, 35,
53, 99
Old Testament 17, 21, 24,
27, 42—43, 45, 53, 56,
61, 70
source and norm 63—64
Seneca 79, 82, 84

Sin and forgiveness 28, 46,
73—74, 110—111; *see
also* Atonement; Baptism;
Communion; Eucharist;
Logos theology; Recapit-
ulation theory; Repen-
tance, public
Slave[s], [ry] 72, 75, 78—80,
85, 96, 123
Sunday 18, 31—32, 37, 38,
99—101; *see also* Agape;
Baptism; Communion;
Eucharist; Liturgy
Tacitus 20, 89, 90, 116—117
Tatian 23, 76, 83, 94, 96
Tertullian 2, 22, 36, 38, 39,
41, 47, 50, 53, 56, 62, 63,
65, 68, 73, 74, 75, 76, 77,
78, 84, 85, 91, 92, 93, 94,
95, 96, 111—113
Tradition[s], [al]
apostolic 52—54, 56—57
Christian 22
ecclesiastical 19, 33, 42
Jewish 17
oral 53—54, 98—99
various religious 20
written 53—54, 98—99
Valentine 20, 21
War[s] 13, 17, 18, 22, 77—78,
85, 94